はじめに

　本書は、ニュース動画を通して現代社会が抱える様々な問題についての理解を深めながら、総合的な英語力を伸ばしていくことを目指したテキストです。現代の国際社会のキーワードである「SDGs（Sustainable Development Goals: 持続可能な開発目標）」の知識を足掛かりに、エネルギーやリサイクルの問題などを中心に世界の様々な課題について学べ　　　　デザインされています。

　本書は、既刊の『SDGs and Global Is　　　　　　　　』と同様のコンセプトで作成したものですが、取り上げている　　　　　　　　ストの内容に重複はありません。年数が経っても陳腐化しない　　　　　　　り学習が終わった後でも折に触れて内容を見返し、社会問題に　　意識を高めることができる内容となっています。

　学習者のみなさんには、英語力を伸ばすことはもちろん、日ごろ意識する機会が不足している自国以外の問題にも関心を持ち、主体的な学習へと発展させ、視野を広げて考え行動することができるようになってほしいものです。本書がその一助となれば幸いです。

　本書の各ユニットは、主にニュース動画に関連する内容のリーディングテキストとニュース動画から成り立っています。主要な内容は次のようになっています。

⏩ Warm Up Quizzes ------------------------------

単文の穴埋め問題を通して、各ユニットの内容と関わりの深い SDGs について学びます。

⏩ Reading Activities ------------------------------

続く動画で取り上げられている社会問題に関して、その背景や予備知識、関連する事象などについてリーディングを通して理解を深めます。

▶ Video Activities ------------------------------

動画クリップを視聴し、様々なスタイルの英語を通して現代社会が直面している課題について学び考えます。

⏩ Exchanging Ideas and Thoughts ------------------------------

各ユニットのトピックに沿った会話演習で発信力を伸ばします。

 Further Activity

リーディングや動画で取り上げられている問題と関連の深い SDGs や社会問題などについて英語のウェブサイトを通してさらに知識を深め、主体的な学習へと発展させます。

▼ Copyrights

Cover

The content of this publication has not been approved by the United Nations and does not reflect the views of the United Nations or its officials or Member States. The United Nations Sustainable Development Goals web site: https://www.un.org/sustainabledevelopment/

Video Activities

SDGs and Challenges We Face
CONTENTS

1

Clean Energy Transition 1

― クリーンエネルギーへの移行１ ―

持続可能な社会を実現させるには、二酸化炭素を排出する石炭や天然ガスなどの化石燃料を燃やす発電から太陽光のようなクリーンエネルギーへの移行を進めることが重要とされています。このユニットでは、SDGs の目標 7「エネルギーをみんなに、そしてクリーンに」と目標 13「気候変動に具体的な対策を」に関連する動画を中心に、エネルギー問題や気候変動に関する国際的な協定とその目標についての知識を深め、世界の現状と課題について学びます。

▶▶ Warm Up Quizzes ---------------------------------------

Learn about SDGs and Goal 7 by completing the following statements.

1. 【SDGs】 In 2015, the United Nations established a collection of 17 global goals known as SDGs to _____ many of the major issues plaguing our world today.

   (A) **admire**　　　(B) **address**　　　(C) **anticipate**　　　(D) **adjust**

2. 【Goal】 Goal 7 _____ to ensure access to affordable, reliable, sustainable and modern energy for all.

   (A) **aiming**　　　(B) **aims**　　　(C) **aimed**　　　(D) **has aimed**

3. 【Target】 By 2030, increase substantially the share of _____ energy in the global energy mix.

   (A) **renewing**　　　(B) **renew**　　　(C) **renewable**　　　(D) **renewed**

4. 【Figures】 Thirteen percent _____ the global population still lacks access to modern electricity.

   (A) **of**　　　(B) **in**　　　(C) **on**　　　(D) **over**

United Nations Department of Economic and Social Affairs Sustainable Development　https://sdgs.un.org/goals

▶▶ Reading Activities ····················· 🔊 Audio 1-02

Read the following passage.

❶ The Sustainable Development Goals (SDGs) are 17 objectives to bring peace and prosperity for people around the world, the seventh of which includes ensuring "affordable and clean energy." According to a report by the United Nations (UN), in the two decades from the year 2000 to 2020, the world's ₅ accessibility to electricity increased from 83 percent to 91 percent. [1] However, it is estimated that there are still more than 730 million people who lack access. [2] Thus, greater efforts are needed to achieve this seventh goal, whose additional target is to increase the proportion of renewable energy within the world's ₁₀ total electricity consumption. [3] Renewable energy is that produced by natural resources, such as sun, wind, water, earth, and biomass. These resources are considered renewable or sustainable because they regenerate naturally and are not exhaustible. Renewable energy is also important from the ₁₅ viewpoint of global warming since it does not create emissions of carbon dioxide (CO2). [4] In this sense, SDG 7 is related to SDG 13, which focuses on "climate action."

❷ There are some indicators on which assessments of Goal 13 rely to measure relevant progress. One of those is "total ₂₀ greenhouse gas emissions per year." Global warming affects the world's ecosystems and causes various climatic phenomena, such as heatwaves, droughts, floods, precipitation, and cyclones. The global temperature is already approximately 1.1 degrees Celsius higher than it was in the pre-industrial era. To reduce ₂₅ the risk of global warming, it is considered that greenhouse gas emissions must peak before 2025 and be reduced by more than 40 percent by 2030 to limit global warming to 1.5 degrees Celsius since the late 1800s. This international goal was set in 2015 at a conference held in Paris, France, known as the Paris Agreement. ₃₀

❸ One of the key concepts regarding CO2 emissions is "net

Glossary:

objectives 目標
prosperity 繁栄

ensure 確実にする
decade 10年

estimate 見積もる

lack 欠く、ない

proportion 割合

consumption 消費

exhaustible 使い尽くし得る、枯渇しうる
emissions 排出(量)

indicator 指標
assessment 評価
rely 頼る、～による
measure 計る
relevant 関連のある
phenomena (phenomenon の複数形) 現象
heatwave 熱波
drought 干ばつ
flood 洪水
precipitation 降雨
Celsius 摂氏
era 時代
peak 最大になる
conference 会議
the Paris Agreement パリ協定

zero," which refers to the state where the amount of CO2 produced by human activity and the amount absorbed by or removed from the atmosphere even out. However, the demand for coal, oil, and gas has been increasing and energy-related 35 CO2 emissions in 2021 reached the highest level in human history. According to the UN Office for Disaster Risk Reduction, this trend could increase the number of largescale natural disasters by 40 percent from 2015 to 2030. Having set this international goal to reduce the CO2 emissions was a great step forward; however 40 reducing them in line with the Paris Agreement and increasing the use of renewable energy still has a long way to go.

state　状態
absorb　吸収する
atmosphere　大気
even out　均一になる

UN Office for Disaster Risk Reduction　国連防災機関

Reading Comprehension 1

Read through the text and choose the correct answer.

1. What does the passage describe?

　a) The most important resource of renewable energy

　b) The latest power generation technology

　c) Two different SDGs' objectives that are related to each other

　d) Some corporations that emit a lot of CO2

2. What figures were reported by UN?

　a) The proportion of sustainable energy of the world's electricity consumption in 2000

　b) The increased percentage of electricity accessibility

　c) Power generation efficiency in 1800s

　d) The number of countries and companies that support the "net zero" policy

3. Which one of the following is mentioned as an event caused by global warming?

　a) Overpopulation

　b) Food shortage

　c) Damage to infrastructure

　d) Rain

4. In which positions from [1] to [4], does the following sentence best belong?
　"During this interval, approximately 460 million people were enabled to use electricity."

　a) [1]　　　　　　**b**) [2]　　　　　　**c**) [3]　　　　　　**d**) [4]

Reading Comprehension 2

Answer the following questions in a complete sentence.

1. Name five major renewable energy resources in alphabetical order. (the renewable energy / are / of / five / resources) biomass, earth, sun, water, and wind.

2. Why are clean energy resources considered renewable?

⊙ Video Activities

Watch the video and answer the following questions.

Check the facts in the video: True or False Questions

Circle **T** if the statement is true or **F** if it is false.

1. Burning of fossil fuels is the main cause of carbon dioxide emissions. [**T** / **F**]
2. Coal-fired power plants are trusted more than renewable energy sources. [**T** / **F**]
3. Some successful examples of wind power generation are explained in detail. [**T** / **F**]
4. Transition to renewable energy sources has little to do with funding issues. [**T** / **F**]

Watch the video and choose the correct answer. Read the script if necessary.

1. What can you infer from the video?

   a) Gambia has a strong international influence over energy issues.

   b) Most construction of new coal-fired power plants has stopped in China.

   c) India is known for its high dependency on coal for electricity.

   d) Japan has little to do with issues about coal-fired power plants.

2. What can you tell about the renewable energy sources?

   a) Solar power is cheaper and more reliable than wind power.

   b) Wind power is cheaper and more reliable than solar power.

   c) They are now used more than nuclear power.

   d) Approximately 40 percent of the world's electricity production is now from renewable energy sources.

3. What can you tell about coal-fired power plants?

    a) They were the world's third biggest source of electricity as of 2019.

    b) Renovation of old plants is the key to improve the energy issues in the 21st century.

    c) Most of the new plants will be built in Asian countries.

    d) Asian countries have been replacing coal-fired power plants with clean energy successfully.

Watch the video and complete the script.   🔊 **Audio 1-03**

The 2015 Paris Climate agreement was a moment of optimism. The world had rallied around a common cause: lowering emissions of (^{1}); attempting to limit global warming to 1.5 degrees Celsius. Six years on, climate change is now a climate crisis. The efforts made so far have not been enough.

"Net Zero by 2050, blah blah blah. Net Zero, blah blah blah. Climate neutral, blah blah ₅ blah."

And it's not just Greta Thunberg that thinks so. This map shows the effectiveness of actions taken by (^{2}) to try and keep the 1.5 goal alive. Only Gambia, a tiny nation in west Africa, is doing enough to help meet the target. The biggest driver of global warming are carbon dioxide emissions. And the biggest cause of these emissions ₁₀ is the burning of fossil fuels. We have known this for years. And yet, from 2009 to 2019, the world's consumption of these fuels barely changed. So why are our energy consumption habits so slow to change?

Electricity production is a key issue. In 2018, it was responsible for 40 percent of the world's total CO_2 emissions. Coal-fired power plants produce a third of the world's ₁₅ electricity.

Finding ways to retire these plants and produce cleaner power is a top priority. But where to begin? (^{3}) percent of new coal power stations planned worldwide are in Asia, where electricity needs are growing. Two of the region's biggest economies, ₂₀ India and China, are both highly dependent on coal for their electricity. China has committed to stop funding coal-fired plants abroad. But more than 360 of them are currently under construction in China itself. And electricity shortages in early November pushed Chinese authorities to ramp up coal production by more than one million tonnes. ₂₅

Even though renewable energy sources are now cheaper in many cases, they are not trusted to deliver the power needed in a market where coal is synonymous with energy security. Many also fear catastrophic knock-on effects if coal-fired plants were to cease production, including mass unemployment in the plants and in related sectors. But things have improved. As the costs associated with wind and solar power have decreased, these sources have become more widespread. 30

Renewable energies now constitute the world's second biggest source of electricity. In 2019, more than a quarter of electricity was produced from renewable energy sources. They are now more used than gas and nuclear power, but still lag behind coal, the most polluting energy source. One of the major stumbling blocks in the energy transition is 35 funding. According to the International Energy Agency, to achieve (⁴   ) by 2050, annual investment in clean energy worldwide will need to reach $4 trillion by 2030. That's more than triple the current level.

>> Exchanging Ideas and Thoughts ························

Practice the conversation with your partner. Think about how you can develop the conversation further.

A: Do you know how many coal-fired power plants we have in Japan?

B: Let me guess. About 50?

A: どうやってその数字を思いついたの？

_____

B: 日本には 47 都道府県があるからです

_____ , so one for each.

A: Actually, there are over 160 plants in operation.

B: That many?! But we do not have any power plants in our prefecture, do we?

 Further Activity

(1) Visit the following website to learn more about **Goal 7** and issues with **coal-fired power plants**. Take notes and share some of the most interesting information you find with your classmates. (2) Using your own key words and/or phrases, try Cinii Research or a similar information retrieval system to find some books and articles that are of interest to you. Compare your list of books and articles with your classmates' lists.

Goal 7   **Coal-fired power plants**

2

Clean Energy Transition 2
― クリーンエネルギーへの移行2 ―

気候変動の原因の一つと考えられているのが、二酸化炭素をはじめとする温室効果ガスです。このユニットでは、二酸化炭素の排出を抑えるために現代社会で取り組まれている様々な対策についての知識を深めます。動画では自動車メーカーや航空会社の取り組みと課題について学び、今後見込まれる世界の二酸化炭素の排出量と現代社会が抱える問題について考えます。

≫ Warm Up Quizzes

Learn about SDGs and Goal 13 by completing the following statements.

1. 【SDGs】 Each one of the 17 sustainable development goals has _____ targets to tackle issues in each field.

   (A) **middle**   (B) **multiple**   (C) **municipal**   (D) **misleading**

2. 【Goal】 Goal 13 aims to take urgent action to combat climate change and its _____ .

   (A) **impacts**   (B) **importance**   (C) **inequalities**   (D) **insufficiency**

3. 【Target】 _____ resilience to climate-related hazards and natural disasters in all countries

   (A) **Shorten**   (B) **Weaken**   (C) **Strengthen**   (D) **Lengthen**

4. 【Figures】 From 1880 to 2012, average global temperature increased _____ 0.85°C.

   (A) **in**   (B) **by**   (C) **on**   (D) **for**

United Nations Department of Economic and Social Affairs Sustainable Development   https://sdgs.un.org/goals

⏩ Reading Activities ·············· 🔊 Audio 1-04

Read the following passage about Carbon Pricing.

❶ One of the key measures in tackling greenhouse gas emissions is carbon pricing. Carbon pricing is an approach to discourage CO_2 emissions and motivate investment in renewable energy and clean technologies. Instead of requiring CO_2-emitting companies to follow a particular course of action, carbon pricing 5 takes advantage of market mechanisms and allows emitters, or polluters, to work toward reducing CO_2 emissions on their own.

❷ For example, the government can set an upper limit on CO_2 emissions for each company. [1] When a certain company's emissions are lower than the limit, it can sell the leftover 10 allowance to companies whose emissions exceed the limit. [2] In other words, when a company successfully reduces its CO_2 emissions, it can earn profit. [3] Since this system involves buying and selling a carbon allowance, it is called an "emissions trading system" or a "cap and trade system." [4]   15

❸ Besides the government-driven approaches above, companies are supposed to make efforts to reduce greenhouse gas emissions themselves. Such efforts are called Internal Carbon Pricing (ICP). In ICP, each company sets its own price on a ton of carbon and uses it for the company's decision-making toward energy saving. 20 As of 2020, more than 2000 companies worldwide either already apply ICP or plan to introduce it in the near future, and the number of companies continues to increase. In Japan, about 120 companies in various fields, such as manufacturing, retail, the service industry, food, transportation, infrastructure-related, electricity producers, 25 and bio-technology have introduced ICP, and more than 130 companies plan to put it into effect within two years from 2020.

❹ As of 2022, the internal carbon price varied widely among companies. While some companies price it at less than 10 dollars for every ton of carbon, others price it at more than 100 dollars. 30 To match the Paris Agreement level set in 2015, it is estimated

measure	対策
tackle	取り組む
emission	排出
investment	投資
particular	特定の
emitters = CO2-emitting companies	
upper limit	上限
leftover	残りの、余りの
allowance	枠
exceed	超える
earn	稼ぐ、得る
besides	〜の他に、〜とは別に
above	上記の、上述の
apply	適用する、利用する
introduce	導入する
put into effect	実行する、実施する
vary	異なる、多様である
estimate	見積もる

that the price should be set to approximately 40 to 80 dollars.

❺ Another key phrase in this regard is "RE100." RE 100 stands for "Renewable Energy 100 percent" and is a global project to encourage companies to use only renewable electricity to run ₃₅ their businesses. RE100 member companies may not have achieved 100 percent renewable energy, but they have set the goal and are committed to showing leadership in this matter. The designation usually involves stricter policies and practices. Hence, the number of companies participating in the RE 100 ₄₀ project is smaller than those applying ICP. Internationally, 350 companies have joined the project and are reporting their progress as of 2022, 65 of which are Japanese.

❻ As mentioned above, there are some schemes to tackle CO2 emissions, and taking advantage of such schemes will hopefully ₄₅ lead to a sustainable society in the future.

stand for 意味する、表す

commit to 尽力する、取り組む

hence したがって、それゆえに
participate in 参加する
as mentioned above 上記したように
scheme 計画、体制

Reading Comprehension 1

Read through the text and choose the correct answer.

1. What does the passage describe?

　a) One of the reasons why CO2 emissions has been increasing today

　b) Some examples of successful Japanese companies tackling CO2 emission

　c) A taxation program to discourage CO2 emission

　d) Some schemes to reduce CO2 emission

2. Which is mentioned as an approach to reduce CO2 emission that is driven by the government?

　a) Emissions Trading System

　b) Internal Carbon Pricing

　c) Renewable Energy 100 percent

　d) Science Based Targets

3. What can be inferred about RE100?

　a) It it more popular in foreign countries.

　b) It is commonly applied among Japanese companies.

　c) Not so many companies have introduced it so far.

　d) It involves government subsidies.

4. In which positions from [1] to [4], does the following sentence best belong?

"Conversely, the more a company emits greenhouse gases over the limit, the more it must pay for the emissions."

a) [1]   **b)** [2]   **c)** [3]   **d)** [4]

Reading Comprehension 2

Answer the following questions in a complete sentence.

1. The purpose of introducing carbon pricing is to (CO2 emissions / investment in / and / renewable energy and clean technologies / motivate / discourage).

_____

2. How can companies make a profit from carbon pricing?

_____

⊙ Video Activities ....

Watch the video and answer the following questions.

Check the facts in the video: True or False Questions

 Circle **T** if the statement is true or **F** if it is false.

1. Governments and countries are more responsible for CO2 emissions than corporations. [**T** / **F**]

2. Some airline companies are planning to go 100% electric in the coming decades. [**T** / **F**]

3. Aviation fuel of any kind cannot be considered as sustainable.   [**T** / **F**]

4. The European Union (EU) has worked positively to make good use of carbon pricing.[**T** / **F**]

Watch the video and choose the correct answer. Read the script if necessary.

1. What car manufacturers are mentioned in the video?

    a) Toyota and Nissan

    b) Volvo and Jaguar

    c) Tesla and Volkswagen

    d) Ford and Chrysler

2. What phrase was used in the video that has a close meaning to "carbon neutral?"

    a) Successful reduction of CO2 emissions

    b) Internal carbon pricing

    c) Net zero emission

    d) Renewable Energy 100 percent

3. What does the video indicate?

    a) The CO2 emissions can rise more in the future.

    b) Thanks to carbon pricing, steady reduction of CO2 emissions is projected.

    c) Carbon pricing has no direct impact on consumers' daily lives.

    d) There is only one practical scheme to reduce CO2 emissions.

Watch the video and complete the script. **Audio 1-05**

Many countries have committed to becoming carbon neutral in the coming (^{1}). China and Russia have set 2060 as the goal. India is aiming for 2070. But just as important as countries are companies. What action are they taking?

In the car industry, a widespread switch to electric vehicles is under way.

Leading names like Volvo and Jaguar have committed to going 100 percent electric in 5 the coming decades.

But for now, roads remain crowded with polluting cars.

Consumers still opt for gas-guzzling SUVs, accounting for (^{2}) percent of total car sales in 2020.

Airlines around the world have also pledged to aim for net zero emissions. 10

The International Air Transport Association has set 2050 as the (^{3}).

But this net zero goal is tough to square with projected passenger numbers, which are set to double over the same timeline.

Airlines are placing their hopes in the development of sustainable aviation fuels derived from organic products like cooking oil and algae. 15

But these fuels are four times more expensive than kerosene.

In 2019, they (^{4}) less than 0.1 percent of the fuel used in aviation.

Researchers say it will not be possible to keep global warming below 2 degrees without a drastic reduction in air traffic.

(^{5}) to force companies to reduce their emissions is carbon pricing. 20

It can take the form of a tax on pollution or a requirement to buy emissions permits, which can be traded.

The problem is in the pricing.

A ton of carbon should cost between $40 and $80 to effectively dissuade companies from using fossil fuels.

But worldwide, the price per ton of carbon is under $10 for the vast majority of emissions under pricing schemes.

The European Union has been a pioneer in this field, and wants to extend the scheme to the construction and road transport sectors.

But the knock-on effect is an increase in the cost of living for consumers, with increased 30 likelihood of social unrest.

2020 saw a dramatic drop in CO2 emissions.

But as the world reopens after Covid-19, they are now projected to reach a record high in 2023.

» Exchanging Ideas and Thoughts ------------------------

Practice the conversation with your partner. Think about how you can develop the conversation further.

A: It is good to know that 世界中の企業が二酸化炭素の排出量を減らそうとしている。

_____

B: Right. I did not know that カーボンプライシングから利益を得られる企業がある。

_____

A: It is an interesting scheme. I hope more companies take advantage of it.

B: Do you remember how many companies are participating?

A: More than 2,000 as of 2020, I believe.

B: I bet the number has got bigger since then.

 Further Activity

(1) Visit the following website to learn about **Goal 13**. Take notes and share some of the most interesting information you find with your classmates. (2) Using your own key words or phrases, try Cinii Research or a similar information retrieval system to find some books and articles of interest to you. Compare your list of books and articles with your classmates' lists.

Goal 13

3 Recycling Issues in Developing Countries

― 開発途上国のリサイクル問題 ―

持続可能な社会の実現を考えるとき、人間のさまざまな活動から出るゴミの再利用は避けて通ることができません。廃棄物を埋め立てや焼却処分するのではなく、再生してもう一度利用できるようにすることが大切です。このユニットでは、プラスチックごみのリサイクルの過程と発展途上国でのごみ処理やリサイクルの取り組みについて知識を深め、ゴミ問題やリサイクル問題について考えます。

≫ Warm Up Quizzes --

Learn about SDGs' Goal 12 by completing the following statements.

1.【Goal】Goal 12 aims to _____ sustainable consumption and production patterns.

(A) **ensure**　　　　(B) **insure**　　　　(C) **decide**　　　　(D) **discuss**

2.【Target】By 2030, achieve the sustainable management and _____ use of natural resources."

(A) **perfect**　　　　(B) **efficient**　　　　(C) **organized**　　　　(D) **finalized**

3.【Target】By 2030, substantially reduce waste generation through prevention, _____, recylcing and reuse."

(A) **deduction**　　　(B) **suspension**　　　(C) **reduction**　　　(D) **expansion**

4.【Fact】Unsustainable patterns of consumption and production are _____ cause of climate change, biodiversity loss, and pollution.

(A) **knot**　　　　(B) **root**　　　　(C) **boot**　　　　(D) **plot**

United Nations Department of Economic and Social Affairs Sustainable Development　https://sdgs.un.org/goals

≫ Reading Activities ---------------- 🔊 Audio 1-06

Read the following passage.

❶ We have all been told to recycle our plastic bottles, but have you ever given much thought about what becomes of those plastic bottles after you throw them into the recycling bin? When you put a bottle into that bin, it begins a long journey before it can be repurposed and used again. ⁵

❷ First, the bottles are collected. [1] This starts at the home with you and your family. The bottles your family collect must then be brought to a central location along with the plastic bottles from other homes and stores. These plastic bottles are next brought to a plastic waste recycling plant where the bottles are ¹⁰ sorted by special machines according to their type.

❸ Most plastic bottles are polyethylene terephthalate, more commonly known as PET. [2] But plastic waste recycling plants also deal with other types of plastic, such as high-density polyethylene (HDPE), which is found in bottle caps and other ¹⁵ stronger plastic items. Plastics are also sorted by their color as well as what they are used for. After the plastics are sorted, they are washed to remove any impurities, such as labels and food.

❹ Once the impurities are removed from the bottles, the plastic is shredded in order to break it down into smaller pieces to be ²⁰ processed for reuse. Next, the plastics must be tested for their quality and thickness. [3] This is done by putting the shredded plastic pieces into a wind tunnel so that the lighter, thinner pieces float to the top while the heavier, thicker pieces stay at the bottom. The final step in recycling plastic involves melting ²⁵ the shredded plastic and then crushing it into small plastic pellets or granules. These pellets can then be used to create new bottles or other plastic products.

❺ Like with everything, however, there are both pros and cons of recycled plastic. The main con of recycled plastic is that the ³⁰ quality and durability of the recycled plastic is not as good as

---

plastic bottle ペットボトル

recycling bin リサイクル用ごみ箱
journey 行程
repurposed 転用される

central location （ゴミ）集積所
along with ～と一緒に
plastic waste プラゴミ
sorted 分類される
polyethylene terephthalate ポリエチレンテレフタレート
high-density polyethylene 高密度ポリエチレン

impurities 不純物
label ラベル

shred 細かく切る

thickness 厚さ

thin 薄い

melt 溶かす
pellets 小粒、ペレット
granules 顆粒

pros and cons 賛否、長所と短所
durability 耐久性

new plastic, often called virgin plastic. [4] The process of recycling plastic (washing, shredding, melting, and crushing) causes a loss in the plastic's integrity, which results in a "flimsy" plastic that is prone to breaking more easily than virgin plastic. The 35 obvious pro of recycled plastic is the environmental impact. Plastic takes up to 450 years to fully decompose. Constantly producing new plastic and then throwing it away can have a very negative impact on the environment as the plastic will quickly fill up landfills. Recycling plastic, however, can drastically reduce 40 the amount of plastic that goes into landfills and help to protect our environment.

virgin plastic　未使
　用プラスチック
integrity　質
flimsy　もろい、壊れ
　やすい
prone　なりやすい

fully　完全に
decompose　分解す
　る

landfill　埋め立て地

Reading Comprehension 1

Read through the text and choose the correct answer.

1. What does the passage describe?

   a) How recycling helps protect the environment

   b) The process by which plastic is recycled

   c) The reasons why recycling is important

   d) How plastic bottles are produced

2. What type of plastic are bottle caps made from?

   a) High-density polyethylene

   b) Polyethylene terephthalate

   c) Polyvinyl chloride

   d) Low-density polyethylene

3. How are plastics tested for quality and thickness?

   a) They are shredded into small pieces

   b) They are melted and crushed

   c) They are put into a wind tunnel

   d) They are sorted by color and use

4. In which positions from [1] to [4], does the following sentence best belong?
   "This is important because how the plastic is reused depends on its quality."

   a) [1]　　　　　　　**b)** [2]　　　　　　　**c)** [3]　　　　　　　**d)** [4]

Reading Comprehension 2

Answer the following questions in a complete sentence.

1. Where do plastic bottles go after they have been brought to a central location?

They are brought to a plastic waste recycling plant (are sorted / their type / the bottles / where / according to).

_____

2. What is the main weakness of recycled plastic?

_____

⊙ Video Activities

Watch the video and answer the following questions.

Check the facts in the video: True or False Questions

 Circle **T** if the statement is true or **F** if it is false.

1. Tunisia has many recycling companies. [**T** / **F**]

2. The company African Recycling mostly employs the wives of unemployed men. [**T** / **F**]

3. Tunisian companies have to pay for most waste to be buried. [**T** / **F**]

4. A landfill near the city of Agareb was closed because of toxic fumes, but it was recently reopened. [**T** / **F**]

Watch the video and choose the correct answer. Read the script if necessary.

1. What can you infer from the video?

a) Tunisia is having difficulty finding a solution to their waste problem.

b) Tunisia is sending their waste to other countries.

c) Working at a recycling company in Tunisia is a good job.

d) Tunisia is importing plastic waste from other countries.

2. What can you tell about the waste in Tunisia?

a) Local citizens make a lot of money off of waste.

b) There is not much plastic waste.

c) The landfills are managed well.

d) Both the government and private companies run landfill sites.

3. What is one of the challenges of good waste management in Tunisia?

    a) The people don't like the smell.

    b) Recycling plastic is too expensive for the country.

    c) Not enough Tunisians pay their taxes.

    d) Companies from foreign countries try to monopolize the waste market.

Watch the video and complete the script. Audio 1-07

This is one of Tunisia's few (^{1}) recycling companies. It transforms mountains of plastic into industrial chips or granules. The company, called African Recycling, started in 2009. Today, it employs around 60 people, mostly women whose husbands are unemployed. Indirectly, the company gives an income to more than 200 people.   5

Its owner Tarek Masmoudi has big ideas (^{2}).

"This waste is an added value and we can create many jobs. We have a great lack of plastic waste in Tunisia. Instead of importing this waste from other countries and losing foreign currency, we can use it in Tunisia."

The (^{3}) of waste in Tunisia is buried – at the cost of the taxpayer.   10

"The state is paying about 150 to 200 dinars per tonne to dump this waste in landfills and to transport it. In Europe and in other countries, they see this waste as wealth. Many financiers in Europe have invested in waste to make money."

Now (^{4}) across the country are almost filled up. In the central city of Agareb a site closed down a few months ago after residents complained about toxic 15 fumes. But authorities had no choice than to reopen it after the neighbouring city of Sfax was buried under rubbish. The decision triggered violent protests mid-November where one person died. Walim Merdaci, an expert on the topic, explains the challenge of good waste management.

"If you want to have solutions, you have to have a fixed strategy, without being able to 20 change it. And that's what we had in Tunisia. We've had many changes and each time we come back to the starting point."

There is (^{5}): only a quarter of Tunisians pay housing tax, including a tax on waste.

"If people don't pay to ensure the cost of treatment each time, we will never have a 25 project. And this is the problem we have in Tunisia."

Authorities have opted for a hybrid method of sorting, compacting and composting waste to tackle the issue. But that will only start in two years. Until then, the only recourse for many remains illegal dumping.

>> Exchanging Ideas and Thoughts ┄┄┄┄┄┄┄┄┄┄┄┄

Practice the conversation with your partner. Think about how you can develop the conversation further.

A: 親にいつもリサイクルさせられています。

_____ . How about you?

B: Yes, I grew up recycling. But, to be honest, それがどれだけ重要かよく理解していません。

_____

A: It was my job to separate the recyclables from the rest of the trash, so I actually hated recycling!

B: Yes, we need to not only tell people to recycle but tell them why they should do it. If people understand the importance of recycling, they will be more likely to recycle.

A: Maybe. But I think most people understand the benefits of recycling. I knew it was important, but I just saw it as extra work. Many cities still don't make it convenient to recycle.

B: It is important that local governments support recycling.

 Further Activity

(1)Visit the following websites to learn about **Goal 13** and **recycling**. Take notes and share some of the most interesting information you find with your classmates. (2) Using your own key words and/or phrases, try Cinii Research or a similar information retrieval system to find some books and articles that are of interest to you. Compare your list of books and articles with your classmates' lists.

Goal 13   Recycling

4 Hair Recycling
— 髪の毛で環境を救う —

持続可能な社会を実現するには、人間が出すゴミの問題を避けて通ることはできません。一般的にゴミとして捨てられている切った後の髪の毛も、使い方によっては環境を守ることに役立ちます。このユニットでは、目標9の「産業と技術革新の基盤をつくろう」を念頭に、髪の毛のリサイクル方法やそのための活動、効果的なリサイクルに求められている社会基盤の整備について学び、考えます。

≫ Warm Up Quizzes

Learn about SDGs and Goal 9 by completing the following statements.

1.【SDGs】 Seventeen sustainable development goals contain 169 targets _____.

(A) **in return** (B) **at most** (C) **in all** (D) **for sure**

2.【Goal】 Goal 9 aims to build strong infrastructure and support _____.

(A) **innovated** (B) **innovates** (C) **innovative** (D) **innovation**

3.【Target】 Support domestic technology development, research and innovation _____ developing countries.

(A) **in** (B) **at** (C) **on** (D) **between**

4.【Figures】 One in three manufacturing jobs have been negatively influenced _____ the COVID crisis.

(A) **among** (B) **because** (C) **for** (D) **by**

United Nations Department of Economic and Social Affairs Sustainable Development   https://sdgs.un.org/goals

>> Reading Activities ················· 🔊 Audio 1-08

Read the following passage.

Hair Recycling

❶ When people cut their hair at a barber or beauty salon, it is usually treated as industrial waste. However, if there is a way to recycle cut human hair, it can be treated as a renewable resource. And in fact, human hair recycling is possible. There is a charity 5 program called hair donation. For someone who lost his or her hair due to alopecia or the side effects of disease treatment, some non-profit organizations offer a complementary medical wig made from donated hair. Those who agree to participate in the program intentionally grow their hair long so that it can be 10 cut and donated.

❷ Another interesting attempt at utilizing scalp hair is mixing it in cement and concrete as fiber material. A study found that the appropriate proportion of scalp hair mixed in cement and concrete can improve its compressive strength. Such utilization, 15 however, is still in an experimental stage and has not come to practical use yet.

❸ Expectations for the practical utilization of cut human scalp hair have been rising in an attempt to contribute to a sustainable society, but there are a number of difficulties in developing an 20 effective recycling scheme, including its collection and proper processing.

Oil Spills

❹ Among the environmental disasters affecting sea creatures caused by human activity are oil spills. When oil spills occur in 25 the ocean, it destroys the habitats of ocean animals, fish, and crustaceans and threatens their lives. While we may think that oil spill accidents only happened in the old days, such as the 1970s and 80s when marine technology and engineering was not as advanced as it is today, it is still happening in the 21st century. 30 For example, on July 25, 2020 a Japanese cargo ship, Wakashio,

barber　理容店、散
　髪屋
beauty salon　美容室
industrial waste　産
　業廃棄物

alopecia　脱毛症
side effect　副作用
treatment　治療
agree to　～に賛同
　する

utilize　利用する
scalp hair　毛髪

compressive strength
　圧縮強度
experimental stage
　実験段階

collection　収集
processing　加工、
　処理

environmental
　disaster　環境破壊
oil spill　油流出
habitat　生息地
crustacean　甲殻類
threaten　脅かす

cargo　貨物

became stranded off the coast of Mauritius in the Indian Ocean. [1] The ship was not a tanker and was not carrying oil as cargo, but it leaked oil from its own fuel tank, causing a spill of about 1,000 tonnes of crude oil. 35

❺ [2] One of the worst oil spills in history, the Kuwaiti Oil Fires, was caused by the destruction of onshore oil wells during the Gulf War in early 1990's. [3] Another possible cause of an oil spill is an oil well malfunction or an exploratory drilling accident in the ocean. [4] Since today's world is still heavily dependent on 40 oil, it is important to minimize the risk of oil spills for underwater life and establish safe and effective procedures for cleaning up in case one does happen.

stranded 座礁する
Mauritius モーリシャス
the Indian Ocean インド洋
leak 漏らす
fuel tank 燃料タンク
crude oil 原油
onshore 沿岸の、陸上の
oil well 油田
the Gulf War 湾岸戦争
malfunction 故障

Reading Comprehension 1

Read through the text and choose the correct answer.

1. What is NOT presented in the first passage?

   a) Some difficulties of hair recycling

   b) Application of scalp hair as a constructional material

   c) Free wigs for people who lost their hair

   d) The monthly cost of hair recycling management

2. What is NOT presented in the second passage?

   a) Some oil spill accidents in the past

   b) The number of oil spill accidents in 2020

   c) Some possible causes of oil spills

   d) Negative impact of oil spills on the environment

3. What is indicated about oil spills?

   a) An effective recovering method of oil spill impact has already been established.

   b) The risk of oil spills has greatly reduced in the last 20 years.

   c) If we stop depending on oil, oil spills will no longer occur.

   d) Oil spills could happen even today.

4. In which positions from [1] to [4], does the following sentence best belong?
   "It must be noted that oil from a stranded ship is not the only cause of an oil spill."

   a) [1]   **b)** [2]   **c)** [3]   **d)** [4]

Reading Comprehension 2

Answer the following questions in a complete sentence.

1. What is the purpose of hair donation?

The purpose of hair donation is to help people (due to / who / lost / medical reasons / his or her hair).

2. Besides stranded ships, write two different causes of oil spills.

⊙ Video Activities --

Watch the video and answer the following questions.

Check the facts in the video: True or False Questions

 Circle **T** if the statement is true or **F** if it is false.

1. Cut hair can be one way to help stop environmental disasters. [**T** / **F**]

2. The UK has established the infrastructure for hair recycling. [**T** / **F**]

3. Six hundred hairdressers joined the hair recycling project in the UK and Ireland. [**T** / **F**]

4. It is harder to collect chemical products like dyes and bleaches. [**T** / **F**]

Watch the video and choose the correct answer. Read the script if necessary.

1. Who is Fry Taylor?

   a) A member of hair recycling group

   b) A barber

   c) A politician

   d) A public servant in London

2. How much cut hair was recycled in the first year of the recycling project?

   a) Amount enough to fill a football stadium

   b) 50 kilo grams

   c) 500 kilo grams

   d) 3.5 tonnes

3. What does the video indicate?

a) Using recycled hair in agriculture is very expensive.

b) There are multiple ways for cut hair recycling.

c) The British government has been trying to make a law for hair recycling.

d) Cut hair collected at hair saloon or barber is usually more damaged than hair cut at home.

Watch the video and complete the script. 🔊 Audio 1-09

Did you know your hair clippings could help mop up oil spills?

Fry Taylor collects leftover locks in his London salon.

Putting the hair into a cotton wrap, he shows how it can be used to make booms, to stop environmental disasters.

Fry is a member of the Green Salon Collective, a group which is making hairdressers 5 more eco conscious through recycling.

"You take your boom, place it into the water."

He uses engine oil to show how the boom works on a larger scale.

"As we pass the hair boom through the water, the hair just naturally will absorb the oil and hold on to the oil, that's the important factor." 10

It's a proven method which has been used against real oil spills, but it hasn't been developed commercially.

Fry says the UK lacks the infrastructure to collect and recycle hair and other salon waste, so he's pushing to change that.

"You can petition and lobby all you like for these types of things, but it's like a grassroots 15 thing, it has to come from the people. So eventually I said, well, we're not going to wait another (¹   ) years for governments and councils to have these systems in place, let's just do it ourselves."

600 hairdressers in the UK and Ireland have joined the collective since its creation last year. 20

As part of their subscription price, members receive (²   ) to separate their waste - hair of course, but also PPE, metal, paper and plastics.

Members are also encouraged to collect chemical waste like dyes and bleaches, which can be sent to energy production facilities.

"I knew that there was a lot of product wastage, I knew we used a lot of foil and towels and 25 plastic. I didn't quite realise the enormity of it but also the little things that could make a change."

"We have all of our tint boxes, our tint tubes go in here, our lids go in here and then they're all disposed of, and we move to our zero colour, this is packed, securely fastened and that also gets sent back, which normally would go straight down the sink. So this in itself is incredible."

The collective estimates that the industry produces enough waste each year to fill 50 football stadiums - and the vast majority is still thrown into landfill.

There's another use for hair clippings: garden compost. Hair is an organic material rich in (³　　　) such as nitrogen, which plants need for growth.

Plus, it can also be used to keep in moisture around plants, and to discourage slugs and snails. 35

"The fact that 99 percent of it goes to landfill is terrifying really, because that's a lot of good material that we can use, it's good ingredients."

In its first year, the Green Salon Collective has recycled almost 500 kilos of hair and 3.5 tonnes of metal.

Its founders hope it will continue to grow, and soon expand into countries across (⁴　　　). 40

≫ Exchanging Ideas and Thoughts ---------------------

Practice the conversation with your partner. Think about how you can develop the conversation further.

A: 髪の毛を寄付しようと思ったことがありますか。

_____

B: いえ、ありません。髪の寄付は知りもしませんでした。

_____ What about you?

A: I've heard of it, but have never taken it seriously.

B: It's great if we can help people in need with something we do not need, like our cut hair.

A: Exactly. But I think to donate our hair, it has to be a certain length.

B: Maybe that's true. Why don't we call a barber or hair saloon to see what kind of conditions there are?

 Further Activity

(1) Visit the following website to learn more about **Goal 9** and **hair donation**. Take notes and share some of the most interesting information you find with your classmates. **(2)** Using your own key words or phrases, and try Cinii Research or a similar information retrieval system to find some books and articles of interest to you. Compare your list of books and articles with your classmates' lists.

Goal9   Hair donation

5 Zero Waste Grocery Store
— ゴミを出さない買い物 —

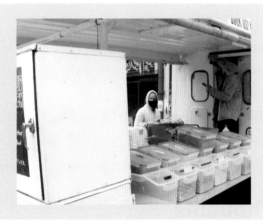

我々の日常生活とゴミは切り離すことができません。埋め立てや焼却、リサイクルなど様々な方法で増え続ける廃棄物に対処していくことが必要ですが、ゴミをできるだけ出さないという姿勢も大切です。

このユニットでは、SDGs の目標 12「つくる責任つかう責任」を踏まえて、プラスチックよりも環境にやさしい代替品やゴミをできるだけ減らす試みについて学び考えます。

≫ Warm Up Quizzes --------------------------------

Learn about SDGs' Goal 12 by completing the following statements.

1.【Target】 By 2030, reduce food _____ along production and supply chains, including post-harvest losses.

(A) **losing**   (B) **lost**   (C) **lose**   (D) **losses**

2.【Target】 By 2030, ensure that people everywhere have the relevant information and _____ for sustainable development and lifestyles in harmony with nature.

(A) **aware**   (B) **awake**   (C) **awareness**   (D) **awaken**

3.【Target】 Support developing countries to strengthen their scientific and technological capacity to _____ towards more sustainable patterns of consumption and production.

(A) **moving**   (B) **moved**   (C) **have moved**   (D) **move**

4.【Figure】 13.3 % of the world's food is _____ after harvesting.

(A) **stolen**   (B) **lost**   (C) **sold**   (D) **bought**

United Nations Department of Economic and Social Affairs Sustainable Development https://sdgs.un.org/goals

Read the following passage.

❶ Much of the world's waste comes from the plastic in which the food and products we buy are packaged. In fact, the world produces over 140 million tons of plastic packaging a year and a third of that ends up polluting our environment. Furthermore, the production of plastic creates 1.8 billion tons of carbon ⁵ emissions every year. It is clear then that plastic is doing a lot of harm to the earth and that something has got to be done to reduce how much plastic is produced and thrown away. [1] One way many companies are taking action is by switching to sustainable packaging options. [2] Sustainable packaging is ¹⁰ made from bio-based polymers and non-toxic wheat or corn materials. An example of sustainable packaging is biodegradable packing peanuts. [3]

❷ Biodegradable packing peanuts are very easy to make so many companies are able to make their own. In fact, even you ¹⁵ can make biodegradable packing peanuts at home by blending corn into a fine paste, mixing it with corn starch, and then microwaving spoonfuls of the mixture. So not only are biogradable packing peanuts good for the environment but because of their simple production method, companies can ²⁰ produce packing peanuts themselves without needing to purchase packing material from a third party. That being said, biodegradable packing peanuts also have several disadvantages.

❸ Even though biodegradable packing peanuts are relatively easy to produce, the production has higher costs than styrofoam ²⁵ packing peanuts. Though the price difference is not big, smaller companies and businesses with a smaller budget may not be able to afford them. Additionally, biodegradable packing peanuts weigh considerably more than styrofoam. This extra weight increases shipping costs, which can become quite expensive for ³⁰ large companies that frequently ship packages.

waste	ゴミ、廃棄物
plastic packaging	プラスチックの容器
end up ~ing	最後には〜になる
pollute	汚染する、汚す
harm	害
switch	切り替える、変える
option	選択肢
non-toxic	無害な
wheat	小麦
corn	とうもろこし
biodegradable	生分解性の
packing peanuts	梱包用緩衝材
microwave	電子レンジで温める
spoonful	スプーン一杯の
production method	製法
styrofoam	発砲スチロール
price difference	価格差
weigh	重さがある
considerably	かなり
shipping cost	運搬料

❹ Biodegradable packing peanuts may also not be suitable for all environments. Because they are made out of a starch, when they come into contact with water, they will dissolve. This means that they begin to break down in humid environments or if a 35 package gets wet. When this happens, they are no longer effective and cannot protect the product.

❺ Though biodegradable packing peanuts may seem like a good option, it is clear they are far from the perfect answer. While it is important to make some sacrifices to protect our environment, 40 we also have to make sure that the actions we take to help the environment don't have too much of a negative effect in other ways. [4] Even though biodegradable packing peanuts can be a great way for some companies to implement more green alternatives and reduce their plastic waste, it may not be 45 appropriate for all companies. In that case, it is important that we keep thinking of new, innovative ways to decrease how much plastic we use and throw away.

starch でんぷん

dissolve 溶ける
humid environment
湿気が多い環境

far from ほど遠い

sacrifice 犠牲

implement 実行する
appropriate 適切
である
innovative 革新的な
throw away 捨て
る、廃棄する

Reading Comprehension 1

Read through the text and choose the correct answer.

1. What does the passage describe?

a) How to package products

b) How to recycle plastic

c) Ways to buy cheaper plastic

d) Ways to reduce plastic waste

2. What is an example of compostable packaging?

a) Packaging made from corn materials

b) Sytrofoam

c) Cardboard boxes

d) Plastic shopping bags

3. What is a problem with biodegradable packaging?

a) They're made of corn so they can become rotten and smell bad.

b) They're not very effective at protecting breakable items.

c) Their production creates a lot of carbon emissions.

d) Their extra weight increases the cost of shipping items.

4. In which positions from [1] to [4], does the following sentence best belong?
"We must carefully consider the consequences of each environmental policy."

a) [1] b) [2] c) [3] d) [4]

Reading Comprehension 2

Answer the following questions in a complete sentence.

1. How much carbon emissions is created from the production of plastic?

(carbon emissions / of / 1.8 / tons / billion) is created from the production of plastic each year).

_____

2. What does the sentence "it may not be appropriate for all companies" mean?

_____

⊙ Video Activities --

Watch the video and answer the following questions.

Check the facts in the video: True or False Questions

 Circle **T** if the statement is true or **F** if it is false.

1. Ella Shone is 32 years old. [T / F]
2. Zero-waste shops have been popular and well-known in London. [T / F]
3. Ella Shone used the phrase "a bit" five times in the video. [T / F]
4. The video is mostly about milk delivery service. [T / F]

Watch the video and choose the correct answer. Read the script if necessary.

1. What can you infer from the video?

   a) The COVID pandemic helped people better understand plastic waste.

   b) Ella Shone lost her job during the COVID pandemic.

   c) Top-up truck became very successful during the COVID pandemic.

   d) Plastic waste is considered as one of the causes of COVID pandemic.

2. When did Ella Shone come up with the idea for top-up truck?

    a) When shopping and noticed all the plastic packaging.

    b) When seeing all the masks on the ground in the park.

    c) When she had a temporary leave of absence from work.

    d) When she was talking about plastic waste problems with her friends.

3. Why does Ella Shone think "we have taken a few steps back"?

    a) People are less aware of the environment than they used to be.

    b) People are producing more waste than they used to be.

    c) People are less likely to recycle now than before.

    d) People are less concerned about recycling or waste problems than before.

Watch the video and complete the script. **Audio 1-11**

"My name is Ella Shone, I'm 32, and I set up a top-up truck last year in lockdown and it is a mobile zero-waste shop that delivers (¹   ) to homes without plastic packaging, that includes bathroom, household and pantry goods."

"The idea came about when I was on furlough leave and I had been thinking a lot about (²   ) reduce the amount of plastic in supply chains and generally waste in supply ₅ chains."

"I thought maybe there's something that we can do around a sort of community shopping experience if you actually take the zero-waste shop to people's doors."

"I think a lot of people aren't even (³   ) the existence sometimes of zero-waste shops or the movement. I mean I think that's thankfully changing and it's becoming a ₁₀ little bit more prevalent and there's other things popping up, but definitely there's a need for it because of the huge amounts of plastic waste that is generated in this country and shipped overseas."

"Nowhere near enough is being done to reduce the amount of waste, so I think there's a lot that needs to be done at (⁴   ) level and at activism level." ₁₅

"It's very straightforward, it's a bit like a go-cart ride but it is a bit stiff on the old steering and it does get a bit bumpy."

"It's a milk float so, ah, it's repurposing something that used to be used for a circular business for another circular business so that's quite nice. But it's also something that is nostalgic so it just seemed like a bit of a no-brainer to do it, to use a milk float. So I ₂₀ just went about trying to find a second-hand milk float online."

"I think there has been a bit of an awakening in terms of our (⁵   ) towards the environment, I think a lot of people have noticed the amount of single-use masks that are lying around the parks and the huge increase in disposable coffee cups that are lying around, and I think we've sort of forked off in some ways and taken a few steps 25 back but that awareness, I think, by and large has got greater."

⫸ Exchanging Ideas and Thoughts ··········

Practice the conversation with your partner. Think about how you can develop the conversation further.

A: 日本では食べ物のパッケージが多すぎると思います。

B: Yes, I think it is a lot compared to some other countries, but 日本の気候のせいで食品はそうやってパッケージされないといけないのです。

A: That is true. I bought some Belgium cookies and they got stale very quickly because they were not individually wrapped like Japanese cookies.

B: Yes, it is a problem. We need to reduce how much plastic we use, but we also don't want to waste food by throwing it away because it goes bad quickly.

A: Good point! I wonder what we can do in Japan.

B: Well, there are other ways we can reduce plastic waste. Let's think of some!

 Further Activity

(1) Visit the following websites to learn more about **Goal 12** and **biodegradable plastics**. Take notes and share some of the most interesting information you find with your classmates. **(2)** Using your own key words and/or phrases, try Cinii Research or a similar information retrieval system to find some books and articles that are of interest to you. Compare your list of books and articles with your classmates' lists.

Goal 12   Biodegradable plastics

6 Plankton with a Global Impact

― プランクトンと環境問題 ―

気候変動や温室効果ガスの諸問題には海洋が深く関わっています。人間の活動によって排出された二酸化炭素を海が吸収することによって、大気中の二酸化炭素濃度の上昇が抑えられているからです。海には目に見えないほど小さな微生物が生息しており、その生態を観察することで気候問題の理解が深まると考えられています。このユニットではプランクトンの生態やその研究について学び、環境問題について考えます。

≫ Warm Up Quizzes

Learn about SDGs and Goal 14 by completing the following statements.

1.【SDGs】 Many of the sustainable development goals require significant funds in order to be successfully _____.

(A) **reaching**　　　　(B) **reaches**　　　　(C) **reached**　　　　(D) **to reach**

2.【Goal 14】 Goal 14 "Life Below Water" aims to conserve marine resources and use them _____.

(A) **sustains**　　　　(B) **sustainably**　　　　(C) **sustaining**　　　　(D) **sustainment**

3.【Target】 By 2025, prevent and significantly reduce marine _____ of all kinds.

(A) **polluted**　　　　(B) **pollutes**　　　　(C) **polluting**　　　　(D) **pollution**

4.【Figures】 An estimated 25,000 tons of _____ has steadily entered the global ocean.

(A) **scrapped ships**　　(B) **dead fish**　　(C) **plastic waste**　　(D) **sewage**

United Nations Department of Economic and Social Affairs Sustainable Development　https://sdgs.un.org/goals

⏩ Reading Activities ⸺⸺⸺⸺⸺⸺ 🔊 Audio 1-12

Read the following passage about plankton.

❶ When considering climate change or global environmental issues, we tend to think that we humans are the key player. It may not be us, however, but plankton, microscopic underwater creatures, that will be deciding the fate of the planet.

❷ Plankton is a Greek word meaning "wanderer" because they ₅ do not swim like fish but seem to drift with the current. [1] Plankton are divided into two major groups: phytoplankton and zooplankton. Phytoplankton are single-cell plants, "phyto" meaning "plant" in Greek. [2] There are more than 5,000 different kinds of marine phytoplankton in the world, typically drifting in ₁₀ the upper 50 meters of the water column where enough sunlight can reach for photosynthesis. [3] Since phytoplankton are very small and grow rapidly, they are the first link in the marine food chain. [4]

❸ As for zooplankton, "zoo" comes from the Greek word "zoon," ₁₅ meaning "animal." Broadly, zooplankton encompass all sorts of tiny creatures. Some of them – for example, copepods – are permanently plankton and belong to a particular category of zooplankton called holoplankton. Others are larval stages of shrimps and crabs that later mature into larger sea creatures ₂₀ and are no longer categorized as plankton. These temporary plankton are called meroplankton. Zooplankton feed on phytoplankton, and zooplankton are also eaten by other small creatures. Thus, their existence in the food chain is critical to the natural environment and underwater biodiversity. ₂₅

❹ A well-known phenomenon caused by plankton is red tide. When a bloom of a certain species of phytoplankton occurs, their fast reproduction results in too many, turning the water a reddish color. Often, red tide depletes oxygen from the water, negatively impacting the surrounding marine environment. ₃₀

❺ From the perspective of climate change, it is not an

---

issue 問題
tend to ～する傾向
 がある、～しがちで
 ある
microscopic 非常
 に小さな
underwater 水中
fate 運命、行く末
wanderer さまよう
 者、放浪者
drift 漂う、漂流する
current 海流
divide 分ける
phytoplankton 植
 物プランクトン
zooplankton 動物
 プランクトン
photosynthesis 光
 合成

encompass 含む、
 包括する
copepod カイアシ
 類 (小型の甲殻類)

larval 幼生 (の)

no longer もはや
 ～ない
temporary 一時的な

biodiversity 生物
 多様性
phenomenon 現象
red tide 赤潮
bloom 大発生
deplete 消耗する、
 激減させる
perspective 見方、
 考え方

exaggeration to say that phytoplankton play one of the most important roles. Oceans are the main absorber of atmospheric carbon dioxide (CO_2), and it is marine phytoplankton that undertake half of the world's photosynthesis. Plants, 35 phytoplankton, and some bacteria produce oxygen and energy from the sunlight, water, and CO_2. While companies around the world are trying to reduce CO_2 emissions through internal carbon pricing or other frameworks, phytoplankton absorb it for free. In addition, particular phytoplankton blooms are affected 40 not only by light and nutrients in the water but also by elevated CO_2 levels in the atmosphere, thus monitoring their ecology could help us understand what is happening to our planet.

exaggeration　誇張
atmospheric　大気中の

undertake　請け負う

affect　影響する
nutrient　栄養素
elevated　（数値が）高い
monitor　観察する、監視する
ecology　生態

Reading Comprehension 1

Read through the text and choose the correct answer.

1. What is true about phytoplankton and zooplankton?

   a) Phytoplankton are capable of swimming like fish.

   b) Phytoplankton grows into zooplankton.

   c) Zooplankton carries out photosynthesis.

   d) Zooplankton preys on phytoplankton.

2. What is mentioned about plankton and their bloom?

   a) Observing their ecology is important to understand climate issues.

   b) Their ecology has a significant impact on aquafarming.

   c) They are a major source of biofuel.

   d) Few researchers have investigated them.

3. What does NOT affect plankton bloom?

   a) Carbon dioxide (CO_2) in the atmosphere　　**b**) Nutrients in the water

   c) Sunlight　　**d**) Seaweed density

4. In which positions from [1] to [4], does the following sentence best belong?
   "That means phytoplankton serve as food for other small marine creatures, such as anchovies, sardines, oysters, clams, and other shellfish."

   a) [1]　　　　**b**) [2]　　　　**c**) [3]　　　　**d**) [4]

Reading Comprehension 2

Answer the following questions in a complete sentence.

1. Why are plankton called "wanderers" in Greek?

Because (drift / the current / they / with).

_____

2. How does red tide have a bad influence on the marine environment?

_____

⊙ Video Activities

Watch the video and answer the following questions.

Check the facts in the video: True or False Questions

 Circle **T** if the statement is true or **F** if it is false.

1. "Microscopic life" and "microorganisms" mean the same thing in the video.   [**T** / **F**]

2. "Silk scrolls" means the data from the research on ocean environment.   [**T** / **F**]

3. The relationship between climate change and oceans has been studied for 90 years. [**T** / **F**]

4. Both phytoplankton and zooplankton play an important role in the marine food chain. [**T** / **F**]

Watch the video and choose the correct answer. Read the script if necessary.

1. In the video, the phrase "teeming under the wave" is closest in meaning to

   a) So many life forms in the water

   b) Some marine creatures making a colony

   c) Small fish living together in the ocean

   d) Some marine creatures that grows very fast

2. Where do planktons like to move to in the ocean?

   a) Warmer areas

   b) Cooler areas

   c) Deeper areas

   d) Nutritious areas

3. What is indicated about the total quantity of phytoplankton in the future?

   a) It is going to gradually decrease first, then rapidly increase later.

   b) It is going to increase.

   c) It is going to remain the same.

   d) It is going to decrease.

Watch the video and complete the script.　　　📶 **Audio 1-13**

Just off the shores of Plymouth, in the south west of England, this research
(¹   ) is hoping to collect a sample of the microscopic life that is teeming below the waves.

Scientists use a "Continuous Plankton Recorder" or CPR, which they submerge under water and tow behind their boat.

Once it's hauled back out of the water, marine scientist Clare Ostle looks to see if they ₅ have caught any of the microorganisms on the silk scrolls within.

"You can see a little bit of green coloration on the silk, that's the phytoplankton in the sample, and if we were to look under a microscope, would see all sorts of zooplankton and phytoplankton, lots of different (²   ) in the water column."

For 90 years, CPR machines have been towed behind hundreds of boats in every ₁₀ ocean, studying the equivalent of nearly 400 circumnavigations of the planet.

In the last few years, scientists have been using the data to see how climate change has been affecting our oceans.

"Taking these samples is hugely important, particularly because we have such a long time series. So, particularly because we're able to look at the trends over at least 30 years, so now we ₁₅ have 60 years, up to 90 years of consistent data, we can see trends in warming in the changes in the acidity of the oceans, how that's impacting food webs, which new species are coming into the area. So these are the kind of (³   ) that we are looking at."

Back on dry land, scientists look through the samples and identify the different species of plankton they collected.　　　₂₀

There are two main types: phytoplankton, diverse plant-like cells commonly called algae; and zooplankton, animals like krill and the larvae of fish, crabs and other marine creatures.

Both are crucial players in the ocean's food chain, but phytoplankton are also behind nearly half of the world's oxygen and helps trap at least a quarter of CO_2 emitted by burning (⁴   ).

But, like many marine animals, plankton have been on the move, heading for cooler ₂₅ areas like the earth's poles. Smaller warm water plankton are also replacing the more nutritious cold water ones, meaning the species that feed on them need to adapt or move too.

"If you think about (^{5}) and a warming ocean, we've seen that that can have direct rapid responses on the plankton, particularly the zooplankton, causing them ₃₀ to change in their seasonality, causing them to change in their nutritional quality, and the areas where you find them, so we're tending to find that they're shifting out of their normal ranges which has an impact on fish that like to eat them."

According to a leaked report by the UN's Intergovernmental Panel on Climate Change due to be published next year, the total quantity of phytoplankton is predicted to fall by ₃₅ around 1.8 to 6 percent over the next century depending on greenhouse gas emissions.

Because of plankton's outsized importance, even such modest reductions could mean an eventual loss of up to 17 percent of marine life.

≫ Exchanging Ideas and Thoughts ---------------------

Practice the conversation with your partner. Think about how you can develop the conversation further.

A: 二種類のプランクトンがいることは知りませんでした。

B: Me, neither. どちらが環境にとってより大切かわかりますか?

A: I think it is phytoplankton.

B: Why is that?

A: Because they are the first in the marine food chain. Zooplankton eat phytoplankton, don't they?

B: Maybe you're right. That means zooplankton depend on phytoplankton.

Further Activity

(1) Visit the following website to learn more about **Goal 14**. Take notes and share some of the most interesting information you find with your classmates. (2) Using your own key words and/ or phrases, try Cinii Research or a similar information retrieval system to find some books and articles that are of interest to you. Compare your list of books and articles with your classmates' lists.

Goal 14

7 Climate Frontline: Sink or Swim
— 後がない気候変動問題 —

石炭や石油、天然ガスなどによる火力発電によって排出される温室効果ガスが地球の温暖化を引き起こし、そのために気候変動の問題がより深刻になっていると考えられています。

このユニットでは SDGs の目標 13「気候変動に具体的な対策を」を踏まえて、気候変動による海面上昇への対策や南アフリカの首都であるケープタウンの実例について学び、人間の活動と自然環境への影響について考えます。

⨠ Warm Up Quizzes -

Learn about SDGs' Goal 13 by completing the following statements.

1.【Goal】 Goal 13 'Climate Action' aims to take _____ action to combat climate change and its impact.

(A) **urgent**   (B) **agent**   (C) **intelligent**   (D) **contingent**

2.【Target】 Strengthen resilience and adaptive capacity to climate-related _____.

(A) **rewards**   (B) **safeguards**   (C) **scorecards**   (D) **hazards**

3.【Figure】 Sea level will _____ 30 to 60 centimeters by 2100.

(A) **rises**   (B) **rise**   (C) **rising**   (D) **have risen**

4.【Figures】 Medium to large scale _____ will increase 40% from 2015 to 2030.

(A) **disasters**   (B) **clusters**   (C) **ministers**   (D) **boosters**

United Nations Department of Economic and Social Affairs Sustainable Development   https://sdgs.un.org/goals

≫ Reading Activities ·················· 🔊 Audio 1-14

Read the following passage.

❶ Climate change is something that affects us all, but many of us are not in immediate danger from it. [1] Research suggests that as early as 2100, up to 60 percent of oceanfront communities will be experiencing chronic flooding, and even today many coastline areas are already feeling the effects. [2] Many coastal ⁵ cities have begun to install barriers, such as sandbags or seawalls. And while this might seem like a simple, effective solution, they are not always reliable. In 2005, for example, a devastating hurricane hit New Orleans and the walls that were supposed to protect the city failed, causing 80 percent of the city ¹⁰ to be flooded and countless lives lost. [3] But, even when these barriers do hold up, they can have unintentional consequences on the natural habitats around these coastal areas. Fortunately, there are other options. [4]

❷ Living shorelines is one way that we can protect our cities as ¹⁵ well as the environment. While seawalls are considered "hard" defenses, living shorelines are what is called a "soft" barrier. Unlike hard defenses that simply deflect and redirect flood waters, a soft barrier is designed to dampen and absorb. Salt marshes fortified with natural materials such as oyster shells is ²⁰ an example of a living shoreline. Mangroves can also be planted along the coast to help protect it. Both marshes and mangroves trap and hold organic matter. As they trap this matter, they continue to grow higher providing protection against the rising shorelines. This is why they are called "living"—they grow and ²⁵ change with the environment.

❸ While living shorelines seem to be an effective measure against flooding of coastline cities, the increased amount and frequency of rain around the world due to climate change is resulting in more localized and riverine flooding. One way to ³⁰ mitigate these types of flooding is through green infrastructure.

---

immediate danger
差し迫った危険
as early as 2100
早ければ 2100 年に
oceanfront 海に面
した
chronic 頻発する
flooding 洪水
coastal 沿岸の
sandbag 土嚢
seawall 防潮堤
devastating 破壊
的な
countless 数え切れ
ない
unintentional
consequences
意図しない結果

shoreline 海岸線

deflect そらす
dampen 弱める
absorb 吸い取る
salt marsh 塩沼
fortified 強化された
oyster shell カキの
殻
mangrove マング
ローブ

measure 方法、手段

riverine 川辺
mitigate 和らげる、
弱くする

The asphalt, concrete, and other impervious materials that currently make up our modern urban infrastructure has impeded the natural hydrological cycles of the land, but green infrastructure are natural designs that absorb water and quickly 35 channel it into the ground to prevent flooding. For example, replacing the hard surfaces on the ground that prevent the absorption of water with porous materials that allow the water to be quickly absorbed into the ground rather than collecting and pooling in parking lots and roads is one effective way at reducing flooding. 40

❹ These are just a few ways that we can protect our cities from flooding while not only minimizing our impact on the environment but helping to improve it.

impervious 水を通さない

impede 妨げる、遅らせる

hydrological cycles 水循環

channel 通す

porous 多孔性

pool たまる

minimize 最小にする

impact 影響

Reading Comprehension 1

Read through the text and choose the correct answer.

1. What does the passage describe?

   a) Eco-friendly ways to protect against flooding

   b) The damage caused by a hurricane in New Orleans

   c) The cost of property on the coastline

   d) Why flooding is good for the environment

2. What type of defense are seawalls?

   a) Impervious

   b) Organic

   c) Hard

   d) Soft

3. Why are living shorelines called "living"?

   a) Because a lot of wild life live in them

   b) Because they change with the environment

   c) Because they protect the environment

   d) Because they are made of plants

4. In which positions from [1] to [4], does the following sentence best belong?
   "For people living in coastal areas, however, the realities of climate change cannot be ignored."

   a) [1]   **b)** [2]   **c)** [3]   **d)** [4]

Reading Comprehension 2

Answer the following questions in a complete sentence.

1. What happens to marshes and mangroves as they trap organic matter?

As they trap organic matter, (against / higher and / protection / they grow / provide / rising

shorelines).

_____

2. What is green infrastructure and how does it help prevent flooding?

_____

▶ Video Activities

Watch the video and answer the following questions.

Check the facts in the video: True or False Questions

 Circle **T** if the statement is true or **F** if it is false.

1. Cape Town is a city that is very near the sea.   [**T** / **F**]

2. The poor communities and rich communities in Cape Town are equally
affected by the rising sea levels.   [**T** / **F**]

3. The coast contributes significantly to the economy of Cape Town.   [**T** / **F**]

4. People do not build on the wetland area because it is illegal.   [**T** / **F**]

Watch the video and choose the correct answer. Read the script if necessary.

1. What can you infer from the video?

   a) Cape Town hasn't recently experienced a major flood.

   b) Cape Town is a very wealthy city.

   c) The residents of Cape Town are not so concerned about the environment.

   d) Cape Town is a good vacation spot.

2. How was Ramba's new home destroyed?

   a) By a flood in the area

   b) By the city

   c) By an earthquake

   d) By a hurricane

3. Why does Anton Cartwright say "we're all going to have to sink or swim"?

    a) Because it is important for people who live near the sea to know how to swim.

    b) Because rising sea levels will eventually affect everyone, so we all need to work together.

    c) Because we have to take care of ourselves and not worry about others.

    d) Because there is no way we can prevent flooding.

Watch the video and complete the script.   🔊 **Audio 1-15**

A city built on, and around the sea. With (¹   ) kilometers of coastline, Cape Town is a prime example of an urban metropolis on the front line of the climate crisis. To combat rising sea levels on this beach, the city has installed sandbags. They protect the coastline, and South Africa's economic interests.

"The beach offers huge amount of social value to Cape Town. The coastline contributes ₅ approximately 10 percent to Cape Town annual GDP, so it's a significant contributor to Cape Town's economy, and it's for that reason that we need to look after it as far as possible."

In the Paris Agreement (²   ), the world committed to limiting global warming to plus two degree Celsius. Enough to slow down - but not prevent - its effects.

"What's interesting for mid-century is not just sea level rise, but sea level rise plus, you ₁₀ know, the average worst flood of the year, or plus a 100-year flood, because that's gonna happen in some places. What does sea level rise plus a flood look like?"

A worrying prospect for those who already live in flood-prone areas. Masiphumelele is an informal settlement that is growing bigger by the day. Nokhutula Ramba is (³

) who has just put up a new house.   ₁₅

"This is the room I built for myself. You can take a look inside."

"This is a wetland, you see, I don't have another place where I can build in. You see ?"

The land is (⁴   ) housing, and it is illegal to build there. Yet thousands of people still do it, because there is nowhere else to go. This presents authorities with a conundrum.   ₂₀

"Now that they are there and have occupied those land parcels, we are in a process now where we are engaging with the other two spheres of government, which are provincial government and national government, to see how best we can deal with the situation because we cannot allow people to live in those conditions."

The city's current policy is to pull down newly built homes before anyone moves in. ₂₅ Ramba's new home is destroyed before her eyes. As the demolition team moves on, she will save what she can from the rubble, and start over.

"This is the door I was using, so I'll build this house, as from them going away I'll start it again and I will try to take sand and stones and put the steps in."

Right now not everyone is equally affected by flooding. A few hundred meters from 30 Masiphumelele, you'll find opulent homes overlooking Lake Michelle.

"This consensus has to be forged across a very wide socio-economic spectrum and that's difficult to do, but those conversations, those difficult conversations have to be held... Because ultimately we're all going to have to sink or swim - literally in this instance - together, right." 35

South Africa is one of the most (^{5}) countries in the world. Communities like this one live worlds apart, but in a few years, the rising waters will reach the wealthy too.

≫ Exchanging Ideas and Thoughts ·····················

Practice the conversation with your partner. Think about how you can develop the conversation further.

A: Since Japan is an island country, 海面の上昇がどう影響するのか注意深く考えなければならないね。

_____

B: Yes, I think so too. Right now the main islands of Japan where most of the population lives isn't be affected so much, so ほとんどの日本人はそのことについて考えていないと思う。

_____

A: Maybe you are right, but the southern islands of Japan are already experiencing the effects.

B: Really? I didn't know that.

A: I don't know the details, but I remember watching a show recently that was talking about it.

B: We should research it more and think of ways we can help!

 Further Activity

(1) Visit the following websites to learn about **Goal 11** and **living shorelines**. Take notes and share some of the most interesting information you find with your classmates. **(2)** Using your own key words and/or phrases, try Cinii Research or a similar information retrieval system to find some books and articles that are of interest to you. Compare your list of books and articles with your classmates' lists.

Goal 11   Living Shorelines

8 The Energy Revolution 1
― エネルギー革命 1 ―

代表的な再生可能エネルギーとしては、太陽光、風力、水力などがありますが、次世代のエネルギー源として注目されているのが海の満ち引きを利用した潮力発電です。
このユニットでは潮力発電についての基礎知識を学び、持続可能な社会の実現に向けたエネルギー問題について考えます。

≫ Warm Up Quizzes ······························

Learn about SDGs' Goal 7 by completing the following statements.

1.【Target】 By 2030, _____ international cooperation for better access to clean energy research and technology.

   (A) **endeavor**　　　(B) **elevate**　　　(C) **educate**　　　(D) **enhance**

2.【Target】 By 2030, double the global rate of improvement in energy _____.

   (A) **elevation**　　　(B) **efficiency**　　　(C) **enhancement**　　　(D) **engagement**

3.【Figure】 As of 2020, 2.4 billion people still use _____ cooking systems.

   (A) **polluting**　　　(B) **pollute**　　　(C) **polluted**　　　(D) **pollution**

4.【Figure】 Between 2010 and 2019, total renewable energy _____ increased by 25%.

   (A) **consuming**　　　(B) **consume**　　　(C) **consumption**　　　(D) **consumers**

▶▶ Reading Activities ·············· 🔊 Audio 2-01

Read the following passage about tidal energy.

❶ When we think of renewable energy, typical images that come to mind may be solar panels, huge wind turbines, and hydroelectric dams. In fact, wind, water, and solar are the top three major clean energy sources. According to the statistical office of the European Union (EU), Eurostat, wind power generates 36 percent of all renewable electricity in the EU. Hydraulic and solar energy account for 33 percent and 17 percent, respectively. There is, however, another promising renewable energy source: tidal energy. [1]

❷ Tidal energy is produced by the earth's rotation and the gravitational pull of the moon and sun. From the perspective of energy generation, tidal currents caused by the rise and fall of the tide work in the same way that the blowing wind rotates the blades of wind turbines. [2] Experimental projects testing tidal energy have been conducted since the 1920s in the United States and Canada. One of the most famous tidal power plants was built in France in 1966 and is still operating, with a 240-megawatt generation capacity. It looks similar to a dam across the estuary of the Rance River. This type of tidal power plant is called a barrage. Another type is a tidal stream generator, which looks more like wind turbines under the water, with some that float while others are settled on the bottom of the ocean. [3]

❸ Constructing tidal turbines is technically more challenging than wind turbines. Since water is 800 times denser than air, tidal turbines must be durable, resulting in higher construction cost. Another requirement for the practical use of tidal turbines is location. There are two important geographic requirements. First, it must be settled close enough to the shore so that the undersea cable that transmits the generated electricity can be installed. A barrage is usually directly connected to a nearby estuary or bay, easily meeting this requirement. However, if a

typical 典型的な
come to mind 思い浮かぶ、思いつく
huge 巨大な
hydroelectric 水力発電（の）
EU 欧州連合
Eurostat ユーロスタット（欧州連合の統計局）
account for 占める
respectively それぞれ
rotation 回転、自転
gravitational pull 引力
current 流れ
rotate 回す
blade 羽根
experimental 試験的な

estuary 河口
barrage せき止め、ダム

float 浮かぶ
settle on 固定される

denser 密度が高い
durable 耐久性がある
construction 建設
geographic 地理的な
shore 海岸
undersea 海中の
transmit 送る

bay 湾

floating generation device is placed in the middle of the ocean, hundreds of miles of lengthy cable must be installed, which is not realistic for operational reasons. Second, the location must have relatively narrow waterways, so that a sufficiently strong ₃₅ tidal current can be generated. For tidal power plants to run effectively, the average tidal range between low and high must be more than three meters. Once correctly installed, the tidal power generator offers a very promising next generation energy source.

❹ [4] To achieve a sustainable society, more international efforts ₄₀ should be made to research tidal power's influence on the surrounding marine environment and to improve the technology for more effective energy generation and power storage.

device　装置

narrow　狭い、細い
waterway　水路
run　運転する

promising　有望な

surrounding　周辺の
power storage　蓄電

Reading Comprehension 1

Read through the text and choose the correct answer.

1. What is true about Eurostat.

　a) It is a durable device designed for underwater usage.

　b) It is a non-profit organization that supports tidal energy generation.

　c) It deals with statistical data about the EU.

　d) It is a group of researchers.

2. What is mentioned about the United States and Canada?

　a) The United States has better tidal energy technology.

　b) Canada has better tidal energy technology.

　c) Both countries have tested tidal energy since the 1920s.

　d) These two countries have invested more for wind power generation.

3. Why is a barrage in France mentioned in the passage?

　a) Because it has the best power generation efficiency.

　b) Because it is famous for its extreme durability.

　c) Because it caused the worst environmental destruction in France.

　d) Because it is one of the first practical tidal energy facilities in the history.

4. In which positions from [1] to [4], does the following sentence best belong?
　"Tidal energy generation is not the latest technology, newly invented in the 21st century."

　a) [1]　　　　　　　**b)** [2]　　　　　　　**c)** [3]　　　　　　　**d)** [4]

Reading Comprehension 2

Answer the following questions in a complete sentence.

1. Why do tidal power generators have to be positioned close to the shore?

Because (the underwater cable / has to / through / the generated electricity / it / transmit).

_____

2 What are the key factors for making tidal energy generation more practical?

_____

⊙ Video Activities

Watch the video and answer the following questions.

Check the facts in the video: True or False Questions

Ⓣ
Ⓕ Circle **T** if the statement is true or **F** if it is false.

1. There is a crashed spaceship on the Shetland shore.	[T / F]
2. Next to the North Sea, there is the Atlantic Ocean	[T / F]
3. One of the advantages of tidal energy is predictability.	[T / F]
4. There are many energy test sites at Oakney.	[T / F]

Watch the video and choose the correct answer. Read the script if necessary.

1. What is Orbital's O2?

   a) A testing site

   b) A tidal generator

   c) A power storage device

   d) An equipment for drilling an oil well

2. What does the video indicate?

   a) Centuries from now, tidal currents can have different patterns or moves.

   b) There is only one type of practical tidal energy generator.

   c) Fossil fuel facilities have brought little profit to local people.

   d) Tidal energy is more reliable than other renewable sources.

3. What element can be a key to store the tidal energy?

    a) Hydrogen

    b) Oxygen

    c) Carbon monoxide

    d) Carbon dioxide

Watch the video and complete the script.   🔊 **Audio 2-02**

It looks like a spaceship that's crashed to earth. But the thousands of tonnes of wreckage on this Shetland shore, are actually a former oil rig. As the high watermark of the North Sea oil boom recedes, more of these huge structures will be brought here for dismantling. Islanders are wondering what comes next for their economy, which has long been supported by fossil fuels. Some think the energy source 5 of the future isn't (¹   ).

"Over there you've got the North Sea. And behind me you've got the Atlantic Ocean. And every six hours, you've got this battle where each one's emptying into the other. So half a billion tonnes of seawater moves through this site per hour on a springtide."

Orbital's O2 is the world's most powerful tidal generator. Moored off the coast of 10 Orkney, the turbine can produce enough electricity for (²   ). But this is far from the first tidal power experiment. Some of those that failed are still visible in Orkney's coastal waters. Orbital think they'll be different.

"Loads of machines have been tested, some of them haven't gotten over the line, and some of them have. And that's what the test site's for. So we end up with a product, the 15 O2, behind us, which we think is ready. We're (³   ) it. We're making power with it right now. And we think that this, this product is scalable."

Another device is being tested in the green gloom beneath Shetland's waves. Nova Innovation's turbines take tidal power from the sea floor to electric cars on the islands, Harnessing its key advantage over other renewables. 20

"The beauty of tidal energy is that it's totally predictable. So I can tell you tomorrow or 2,000 years from now, how much tide is going to be flowing through that channel out there, our energy resource is not (⁴   ) the weather, it's slightly influenced by it, but basically, it's predictable."

Those all important tides may be regular but they only come in and out twice a day. 25 Luckily the Northern Isles are an ideal testing ground for exploring innovative ways to store that energy.

"A lot of people describe Orkney as a living laboratory. We have lots of test sites, and various different companies that are all working together in this sort of green economy."

The European Marine Energy Centre, based here, thinks hydrogen could be one answer. Researchers convert the tidal energy into hydrogen, which can then be stored and turned back into (^{5}) whenever it's needed. It's already powering these ferries when they dock overnight and the hope is to see this proof of concept could work on a bigger scale.

≫ Exchanging Ideas and Thoughts ----------------------

Practice the conversation with your partner. Think about how you can develop the conversation further.

A: 太陽エネルギーが一番人気がある再生可能エネルギーだと思っていました。

_____

B: EU では風力発電が 2 倍発電していますね。

_____

A: That's right. Actually, I didn't really know much about tidal energy.

B: I am wondering if there is any tidal energy generators in Japan.

A: Since Japan is surrounded by the sea, we may have many good spots for tidal energy generation.

B: It would be great if Japan can be a leader in technology development for tidal energy generation.

 Further Activity

(1) Visit the following website to learn more about **Goal 7** and **tidal power generation**. Take notes and share some of the most interesting information you find with your classmates. (2) Using your own key words and/or phrases, try Cinii Research or a similar information retrieval system to find some books and articles that are of interest to you. Compare your list of books and articles with your classmates' lists.

Goal 7

Hydropower / Tidal power

9 The Energy Revolution 2

― エネルギー革命 2 ―

温室効果ガスを排出する化石燃料による発電から再生可能なエネルギーへと移行するには、十分な発電量を確保するために多くの施設の建設が必要となります。このユニットでは、目標11「住みつづけられる街づくりを」を踏まえて、クリーンエネルギー導入の際に発電所を受け入れる地域社会の経済や人々の生活への影響について考えます。

≫ Warm Up Quizzes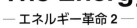

Learn about SDGs' Goal 11 by completing the following statements.

1.【Goal】 SDGs' Goal 11 aims to _____ human cities and settlements safe and sustainable.

(A) **dismantle**　　　(B) **make**　　　(C) **leave**　　　(D) **adjust**

2.【Target】 Strengthen efforts to _____ the world's cultural and natural heritage.

(A) **protection**　　　(B) **protect**　　　(C) **protector**　　　(D) **protecting**

3.【Figures】 Ninety-nine percent of the world's urban population _____ polluted air.

(A) **consume**　　　(B) **breathe**　　　(C) **develop**　　　(D) **absorb**

4.【Figures】 Half of humanity – 3.5 billion people – lives in cities today and 5 billion people are _____ to live in cities by 2030.

(A) **project**　　　(B) **projects**　　　(C) **projected**　　　(D) **projecting**

United Nations Department of Economic and Social Affairs Sustainable Development　https://sdgs.un.org/goals

⏩ Reading Activities ········· 🔊 Audio 2-03

Read the following passage about community acceptance.

❶ Whether solar panels or wind turbines, the development of clean energy facilities is often compared with the electricity generated from fossil fuels, such as natural gas and coal. In reality, how clean energy facilities affect the local community is as important as the performance of renewable electricity 5 generation itself. So what external factors should be considered from the standpoint of the local communities where clean energy power plants will be installed?

❷ When a wind power plant project is developed and introduced to a certain area, there are both positive and negative factors that 10 could have an impact on whether or not the community accepts the new project. [1] Some common positive factors or drivers include the following: (1) Profit and income to the local economy in the form of taxes and job opportunities; (2) individual profits, such as from electricity use, landowner's income, and increased 15 property values; (3) a positive influence on the environment, such as the potential of wind energy to reduce greenhouse gas emissions; and (4) trust built through transparency in the development planning and process. Conversely, there are numerous negative factors or barriers that may turn a community 20 off to wind power. [2] These barriers include: (1) a negative environmental impact on the biodiversity and wildlife around the site; (2) changes in the existing natural landscape; (3) health issues, such as sleep disorders due to the low frequency vibration from the turbines; (4) quality of life; (5) proximity to the facility; 25 and (6) the size of the turbine and shadow flicker caused by the spinning blades, among others. [3] Since the average size of a wind turbine has increased over time to generate more electricity, the psychological impact from its appearance cannot be overlooked. For example, the average height of onshore wind 30 turbines in the United States is over 460 feet or 140 meters,

---

whether A or B　A であれ B であれ
be compared with　～と比べる、比較する
affect　影響する

external　外部の
factor　要因
standpoint　観点、視点

impact　影響
driver　要因、動機
profit　利益
income　収入

landowner　地主
property　所有地

transparency　透明性
conversely　逆に、反対に
numerous　多数の
barrier　妨げ、障害
site　（建設）現場、建設場
landscape　風景
sleep disorder　睡眠障害
low frequency vibration　低周波振動
proximity　近さ
shadow flicker　（風車の羽根による）ちらちら動く影
appearance　外見、見た目

compared to the Statue of Liberty, which is 305 feet tall, or about 93 meters. Clearly, modern wind turbines are monstrous in size, so it is understandable that the subjective well-being or psychological stress of having them in one's sight may underlie 35 the various negative factors of wind turbines. [4]

❸ Since tidal power plants are on the surface or underwater, the related factors are not exactly similar to those of wind turbines, these sorts of renewable energy generators may be preferable. In any case, gaining community acceptance for clean energy 40 facilities is one of the key issues when pushing to replace non-renewable with renewable energy.

monstrous 巨大な
subjective 主観的な
in sight 見える範囲に、間近に
underlie 根底にある
underwater 水中

preferable 好ましい
replace A with B A を B に置き換える

Reading Comprehension 1

Read through the text and choose the correct answer.

1. The word "installed" in paragraph 1, line 8, is closest in meaning to :

  a) introduced

  b) agreed

  c) practiced

  d) researched

2. What is mentioned about drivers and barriers?

  a) Positive factors are more important to local people than negative factors.

  b) Usually there are more drivers than barriers.

  c) Negative factors are more important to local people than positive factors.

  d) Usually there are more barriers than drivers.

3. Why is the size of the Statue of Liberty mentioned in the passage?

  a) To show how tall modern wind turbines are

  b) As an example of impressive appearance

  c) To emphasize the advanced construction technology

  d) To switch topics in the paragraph

4. In which positions from [1] to [4], does the following sentence best belong?
"It was reported that over 20% of wind energy projects are delayed due to criticism and opposition from local communities."

  a) [1]   **b**) [2]   **c**) [3]   **d**) [4]

Reading Comprehension 2

Answer the following questions in a complete sentence.

1. What is one of the health issues related to wind turbines ?

It is (caused / from / low frequency vibration / by / sleep disorder / wind turbines).

_____

2. Why does the subjective well-being of local people have to be taken care of?

_____

⊙ Video Activities ----------------------------

Watch the video and answer the following questions.

Check the facts in the video: True or False Questions

 Circle **T** if the statement is true or **F** if it is false.

1. The Northern Isles' economy has depended on fossil fuels since the 1970s.   [**T** / **F**]

2. The Viking project is not about tidal energy generation.   [**T** / **F**]

3. Five wind turbines at Burradale are installed basically due to local people's demand.   [**T** / **F**]

4. Drilling a new oil field is banned in the UK.   [**T** / **F**]

Watch the video and choose the correct answer. Read the script if necessary.

1. Who is Elaine Tait?

   a) A local resident against the Viking project

   b) A politician from Shetland

   c) The CEO of one of the largest oil companies

   d) A geographical scientist

2. What is one of the local residents' views about renewable energy?

   a) The high cost of installing renewable energy generators has to be overcome as soon as possible.

   b) People cannot depend only on the renewable energy yet.

   c) Clean energy technology has now been advanced enough.

   d) Small islands are more suitable for wind turbines.

3. What is true about COP 26 conference?

   a) It is a domestic conference in the UK.

   b) It could have an affect on the government's decisions.

   c) It is a research project for oil and gas energy generation.

   d) It is held in the UK every year.

Watch the video and complete the script.   📶 **Audio 2-04**

But the Northern Isles' energy future is far from settled. Fossil fuels have fired the area's economy since the 1970s. Shetland still hosts one of Europe's largest oil and gas terminals, which provides high-skilled jobs and amenities for the ([1]   ) islanders. But the fuel that comes in here doesn't keep the Shetlanders' lights on, most of it goes overseas, leaving them to rely on more expensive imports. These five wind 5 turbines at Burradale could signal the start of the islands' energy independence. Across Shetland's central mainland the foundations of over a hundred turbines are now being laid as part of the new Viking wind farm project. These will be able to power all of Shetland with excess electricity being sold to the Scottish mainland.

"We've maybe been delayed somewhat because of how much we've benefited from 10 ([2]   ). So we've maybe become quite used to that business. But now we're slowly moving away and using oil and gas as an enabler to the transitions."

But many islanders question the huge scale of the Viking project, like Shetland pony breeder Elaine Tait.

"Most of the Shetlanders that I know are really against the Viking project. They're not 15 against renewable energy, that is always a good thing. But it just seems to be that there's nothing green about this project. And it's one of the largest wind farms, if not the largest wind farm in Europe, on one of the smallest islands and it doesn't make any sense."

Despite the island's progress harnessing the wind and tides, there remains the question of whether valuable oil and gas should be left in the ground. Greenpeace are 20 among those campaigning against an application to drill a new oil field, known as Cambo. The UK government is set to decide next year after the COP26 climate conference.

"I think we need to leave as much of it in the ground as we possibly can. There is an amount of fossil fuels that we need to use as we taper down to net zero. But I think we 25 cannot continue to just go approving oil and gas fields, as if there isn't a ([3]   ) because there is one."

Others think placing so much reliance on renewables isn't realistic.

"People are in two minds. Should we develop it? Because if we don't develop it, we'll rely more on imports. But even without Cambo, we've got the Clearfield west of Shetland, ₃₀ which is looking to be developed. So oil and gas does seem to be in the mix for at least another 20 to 30 years."

The remains of Neolithic settlements still dot the landscape of the Northern Isles. Those living here now face difficult choices about what kind of legacy they will leave for (⁴   ). ₃₅

Exchanging Ideas and Thoughts --------------------

Practice the conversation with your partner. Think about how you can develop the conversation further.

A: I am not against renewable energy, but 見えるところにはほしくないです。

B: Really? 丘の上の大きな風車ってけっこうかっこいいと思っていました。

A: You have to have some negative feelings about living close to those generators!

B: Well, as long as I do not hear any noise, maybe it's okay with me.

A: Even if you do not notice any sound, they could cause some health issues.

B: Like what?

Further Activity

(1) Visit the following website to learn more about **Goal 11**. Take notes and share some of the most interesting information you find with your classmates. (2) Using your own key words and/or phrases, try Cinii Research or a similar information retrieval system to find some books and articles that are of interest to you. Compare your list of books and articles with your classmates' lists.

Goal 11

10 Bed Linen Recycled into School Shirts
— リサイクル制服 —

このユニットでは SDGs の目標 10「人や国の不平等をなくそう」の観点から、学校の制服を取りあげ、その意味について考えます。また、制服に関連したトピックとして、廃棄される衣類のごみ問題やその再生法、南アフリカで実践されている使用済みのリネンをリサイクルして学校の制服を作る試みについて学び、持続可能な社会の実現についての考えを深めます。

≫ Warm Up Quizzes

Learn about SDGs' Goal 10 by completing the following statements.

1.【Goal】Goal 10 aims to _____ inequality within and among countries.

(A) **change**　　　(B) **reduce**　　　(C) **bring**　　　(D) **increase**

2.【Target】Progressively _____ and sustain income growth of the bottom 40 percent of the population at a rate higher than the national average.

(A) **form**　　　(B) **achieve**　　　(C) **make**　　　(D) **organize**

3.【Target】Adopt policies, especially fiscal, wage and social _____ policies, and progressively achieve greater equality.

(A) **protection**　　　(B) **protect**　　　(C) **protected**　　　(D) **protecting**

4.【Figure】Children in the poorest 20% of the _____ are still up to three times more likely to die before their fifth birthday than children in the richest quintiles.

(A) **areas**　　　(B) **discussions**　　　(C) **education**　　　(D) **populations**

≫ Reading Activities ········· 🔊 Audio 2-05

Read the following passages.

School Uniform

❶ Japanese school uniforms were first introduced during the Meiji Period when Japanese culture began to mix with and become more influenced by Western cultures and styles. The Japanese school uniform has undergone various changes 5 throughout the years to result in today's style. The purpose of the Japanese uniform is to instill a sense of discipline and community among the youth of Japan. While this may be the most commonly stated purpose of uniforms in Japan, the uniform also offers another very important benefit: equality. Today, 10 thousands of schools around the world require their students to wear some type of standardized clothing in an attempt to overcome socioeconomic disparity among students and provide a level playing ground for all. Proponents claim that school uniforms not only bring equality to the classroom but also 15 greater learning. Uniforms mean that students do not need to concern themselves with current fashion trends and the pressures that come with that and can instead keep their attention on their education. Studies have also shown that school uniforms can increase school attendance as well as create a safer 20 environment for students by reducing instances of bullying and school violence.

become influenced
影響を受けた
undergo 経験する

instill 植え付ける
discipline 規律、自
制心

equality 平等
standardized 標準
化された
attempt 試み
overcome 乗り切る
socioeconomic
disparity 経済的
格差
a level playing
ground 公平な条
件
proponents 支持者
current 流行してい
る、現在の
school attendance
出席
bullying いじめ

Recycling Used Clothes

❷ It is estimated that 92 million tons of textile waste is produced annually by the fashion industry largely fueled by today's "fast 25 fashion" trends. [1] It is clear that the social and environmental impact of this waste must be addressed and more companies are moving away from "fast fashion" to sustainable fashion by recycling used clothing rather than simply disposing of it. The most common way clothing is recycled is by a process called 30 mechanical recycling, which is a process by which a fabric is broken

textile waste 繊維
クズ
annually 毎年

fuel 煽る、刺激する
address 対処する
used clothing 古着
dispose of 捨てる、
廃棄する
fabric 織物

59

down into its smaller fibers without the use of chemicals. [2]
First, the fibers are shredded and carded (or separated) from
the fabric. This fiber can then be spun to make yarn that can be
used again to create knitted fabrics. Mechanical recycling is 35
most commonly done with cotton, but many of the fabrics today
are made up of a blend of various materials. [3] In that case,
chemical recycling is used. In chemical recycling, a series of
chemical processes separate blended fibers from one another. [4]
Due to the use of chemicals, this process is not so environmentally 40
friendly, but, unlike mechanical recycling in which the resulting
fibers are weakened through the shredding and carding process,
chemical recycled fibers are just as strong as virgin fibers.

fibers 繊維
chemicals 化学品
shred 細断する
card すく
spun 紡ぐ
yarn 糸
cotton 綿

blended fibers 混紡
繊維

weaken 弱める
virgin fibers 新し
い繊維

Reading Comprehension 1

Read through the text and choose the correct answer.

1. What does the first passage describe?

  a) The negative points of school uniforms

  b) The positive points of school uniforms

  c) How school uniforms are made

  d) How school uniform fashion has changed

2. What does the second passage describe?

  a) Popular fashion brands

  b) Fast fashion

  c) The processes by which clothes are recycled

  d) The best way to recycle clothes

3. According to the first passage, what do proponents of school uniforms claim?

  a) School uniforms make students smarter.

  b) School uniforms are very fashionable.

  c) Japanese school uniforms have the best styles.

  d) Japanese school uniforms improve education.

4. In which positions from [1] to [4], does the following sentence best belong?
  "So mechanical recycling cannot be used to recycle those fabrics."

  a) [1]   **b)** [2]   **c)** [3]   **d)** [4]

Reading Comprehension 2

Answer the following questions in a complete sentence.

1. According to the first passage, what is the purpose of the Japanese school uniform?

The purpose of the Japanese uniform is (a sense of / to instill / among / the youth of Japan / discipline and community).

_____

2. According to the second passage, which recycling process produces stronger fabrics?

_____

⊙ Video Activities

Watch the video and answer the following questions.

Check the facts in the video: True or False Questions

 Circle **T** if the statement is true or **F** if it is false.

1. The hotel in the video is located in Cape Town.   [**T** / **F**]

2. The hotel doesn't throw away their bed linens until they have worn out. [**T** / **F**]

3. One bed sheet can make up to 5 shirts for children.   [**T** / **F**]

4. The COVID-19 pandemic had a major impact on the employment rate in South Africa. [**T** / **F**]

Watch the video and choose the correct answer. Read the script if necessary.

1. Why do people want to stay at the hotel in the video?

  a) Because they are near the ocean.

  b) Because they are environmentally friendly.

  c) Because they want the best.

  d) Because they are free to stay.

2. What can you tell about school uniforms in South Africa?

  a) They are paid for by the government.

  b) They are a source of inequality among students.

  c) Uniforms help to erase differences in social class.

  d) They are designed by students themselves.

3. What does a new shirt do for a child?

    a) A new shirt helps a child feel more confident.

    b) A new shirt makes a child feel uncomfortable.

    c) A new shirt makes a child think more about their differences.

    d) A new shirt represents the independence of the community.

Watch the video and complete the script.   📶 **Audio 2-06**

This (^{1}) hotel with views over Cape Town draws clients who want the best. This starts with the bed linen, thrown out well before it wears through. But it can have a second life.

"We found the project of Restore SA through a linen supplier that we use now for Parker Cottage and we are giving them the old linen now, to make school shirts."   5

The project (^{2}) Restore SA transforms linen into school shirts. More than a hundred thousand children have been clothed (^{3}). When old linen is collected, it ends up in this workshop. A single bed sheet has enough material for five shirts in a vastly unequal country where school uniforms are compulsory. The project is the brain child of Danolene Johanessen, who believes that no child should leave home 10 in rags.

"So we wanted look at a way how do we keep our children in school, how do we get them dressed for school and how do we just, you know, to boost 15 their self-esteem."

It is an (^{4}) that school uniforms, meant to erase differences in social class, cost much too much for South Africa's poor. All the more so after the Covid-19 pandemic, and unemployment passing 20 (^{5}). So the shirts are (^{6}) to mothers like Lemiese Pieterse, who lives with her family in a township 200 kilometers west of Cape Town.

"Today I came here to collect a shirt for my daughter and I am very blessed."

With fresh linen and loving tailoring, the shirts can hold up to the best – even those straight from the shop.   25

≫ Exchanging Ideas and Thoughts ---------------------

Practice the conversation with your partner. Think about how you can develop the conversation further.

A: 母親が制服を買ってくれたのを覚えています。

_____ when I was in school.

I didn't think about the price, but now I know they are very expensive.

B: Yes, they are very expensive! I read that a complete set of winter, summer, and athletic uniforms can cost as much as 100,000 yen!

A: How can low-income families afford that?

B: 多くは買えないと思います。_____

But in recent years some school's PTAs have started to help provide uniforms to families who cannot afford them by collecting uniforms from graduates who no longer need them.

A: Oh, that is a good idea! There are many ways to "recycle" clothes, aren't there?

B: Yes! Certainly donating your used clothes that are still in good condition is a good way to support others in need as well as help protect the environment.

Further Activity

(1) Visit the following websites to learn more about **Goal 10** and **recycling**. Take notes and share some of the most interesting information you find with your classmates. **(2)** Using your own key words and/or phrases, try Cinii Research or a similar information retrieval system to find some books and articles that are of interest to you. Compare your list of books and articles with your classmates' lists.

Goal 10

Recycling

11 Agriculture in a Developing Country
― 開発途上国の農業 ―

現代社会が抱える問題の多くはSDGsの目標どれか一つにだけに当てはまるものではなく、複数の領域が関わっていることが通例です。このユニットでは、目標2「飢餓をゼロに」と目標9「産業と技術革新の基礎をつくろう」などに関わる事例として、アフリカ大陸の中央アフリカ共和国を取りあげ、人々の暮らしや国の経済発展の問題に関して学び、考えます。

≫ Warm Up Quizzes

Learn about SDGs' Goal 2 and 9 by completing the following statements.

1.【Goal】 Goal 2 aims to end hunger, achieve food security, improve nutrition and _____ sustainable agriculture.

(A) **promotes**　　　(B) **promote**　　　(C) **promoted**　　　(D) **promoting**

2.【Target (Goal 2)】 By 2030, double the agricultural _____ and incomes of small-scale food producers.

(A) **productive**　　　(B) **produce**　　　(C) **producing**　　　(D) **productivity**

3.【Goal】 Goal 9 aims to build resilient _____ , promote inclusive and sustainable industrialization and foster innovation.

(A) **aquaculture**　　　(B) **mixture**　　　(C) **texture**　　　(D) **infrastructure**

4.【Target (Goal 9)】 Support domestic technology development, research and innovation in _____ countries.

(A) **developed**　　　(B) **develop**　　　(C) **developing**　　　(D) **to develop**

United Nations Department of Economic and Social Affairs Sustainable Development　https://sdgs.un.org/goals

⏩ Reading Activities ·············· 🔊 Audio 2-07

Read the following passage about community acceptance.

❶ There are few countries in the world whose name explains exactly where to find it on a map. Japan is in Asia, Germany in Europe, and Jamaica in the Caribbean — but nothing in their names indicates where on Earth they actually are. However, the Central African Republic (CAR) is exactly where the name suggest it might 5 be — at the heart of the world's largest continent. The landlocked nation is the 44th biggest in the world but has a population of only 5.5 million people. It is also one of the poorest countries in the world. With an average salary per person of just US$448, the CAR is ranked 212th out of 216 countries in the world. [1]   10

❷ The United Nations has also declared the Central African Republic as the least developed nation in the world. [2] Yet, the tragedy for the citizens of the CAR, is that its population really should not be so poor. Amongst its plentiful natural resources include uranium, crude oil, gold, diamonds, cobalt, lumber, and 15 hydropower. Principal cash crops include cotton, coffee, and tobacco. The biggest problem for the CAR is that although diamonds account for 61 percent of the country's export sales, it is estimated that between 30 percent to 50 percent are smuggled out of the country illegally.   20

❸ The country is also home to the second largest rainforest in the world — the Congo Basin, which teems with abundant nature and wildlife. The rainforest is home to 10,000 species of tropical plants, 1,000 types of birds, 700 kinds of fish and 400 species of mammals — including forest elephants, chimpanzees, 25 and mountain gorillas. [3] Yet, similar to the Amazon Rainforest in South America, each decade has seen the size of the Congo Rainforest decrease through human commercial activity.

❹ The term 'conflict diamonds' is well-known; it refers to diamonds that have been illegally removed from a company 30 usually by rebel military groups using stolen children as soldiers.

indicate　示す
CAR　中央アフリカ共和国
heart　中心
continent　大陸
landlocked　内陸の

per person　一人当たり
ranked　順位付けられている
declare　宣言する
tragedy　悲劇
citizen　国民、人民
amongst　の中に
plentiful　豊富な
natural resource　天然資源
crude oil　原油
cash crops　換金作物

smuggle　密輸する
illegally　違法に

Congo Basin　コンゴ盆地
teem　満ちる、富む
abundant　豊かな
mammal　哺乳類
similar to　に似ている、と同じように
commercial activity　商業活動

term　言葉

rebel military group　武装反乱グループ

[4] The CAR is home to the largest illegal export of timber in the world. The export every year of thousands of illegal tons of timber from the Congo Basin results in hundreds of millions of dollars in lost revenue for the CAR. Money that could be used to 35 help fight poverty, improve education and build infrastructure such as roads that could help transform the lives of the citizens.

❺ Hope remains that the future can be brighter than the CAR's darker past. As US State Department Deputy Assistant W Stuart Symington has said, "It is time to break the cycle of suffering, to 40 align this day of opportunity with tomorrow. Changing lives so that occupants become citizens, and citizens change their countries."

export　輸出

revenue　歳入、収益

US State
　Department
　Deputy Assistant
　アメリカ国務省次官補
align　足並みをそろ
　える、整える
occupants　居住者

Reading Comprehension 1

Read through the text and choose the correct answer.

1. What is mentioned about the country name, the Central African Republic?

　a) It is the longest country name in the African Continent.

　b) It has been revised multiple times through history.

　c) It represents the location of the country.

　d) It was named by another country in the African Continent.

2. What is NOT mentioned as a natural resource in the CAR?

　a) Lumber　　　　**b)** Silver

　c) Gold　　　　　**d)** Uranium

3. What is true about diamonds and timber produced in the CAR?

　a) Timber is more lucrative than diamonds in the CAR.

　b) Economic development of the CAR has been disturbed by illegal trading of these products.

　c) CAR needs to develop processing technology for both of them.

　d) CAR has a rich timber resource but does not produce diamonds at all.

4. In which positions from [1] to [4], does the following sentence best belong?
"What is less widely known is the international trade in 'conflict-timber."

　a) [1]　　　　**b)** [2]　　　　**c)** [3]　　　　**d)** [4]

Reading Comprehension 2

Answer the following questions in a complete sentence.

1. How has the United Nations described the CAR?

The United Nations described the CAR as (in / nation / the least / the world / developed).

_____

2. What is an important feature of the CAR from the viewpoint of global ecosystem?

CAR has _____ .

⊙ Video Activities ·

Watch the video and answer the following questions.

Check the facts in the video: True or False Questions

 Circle **T** if the statement is true or **F** if it is false.

1. The Central African Republic has one of the best economies among the African nations. [**T** / **F**]

2. There are some private investors trying to make agriculture in the CAR better.   [**T** / **F**]

3. Food aid programs have helped the CAR's citizen and economy a lot.   [**T** / **F**]

4. Environmentalists have helped private investors to develop the cultivation of palm oil. [**T** / **F**]

Watch the video and choose the correct answer. Read the script if necessary.

1. What is a problem many people in the CAR have been facing?

   a) Poor hygiene

   b) Insufficient food

   c) Small number of elementary schools

   d) Natural disasters

2. What is indicated in the video?

   a) Building factories and warehouses is more efficient to develop the the CAR economy.

   b) Regenerative agriculture and sustainable agriculture are two different agricultural forms.

   c) Soil in the CAR is not suitable for agriculture and advanced technology is required to have better agricultural practice.

   d) Not all investors support the sustainable agriculture approach.

3. What is the key to protect and develop the CAR industry?

   a) Manufacturing of processed products

   b) Prevention of soil contamination

   c) Providing better educational opportunities

   d) Development of social welfare system

Watch the video and complete the script.

 Audio 2-08

A truck laden with commercial crops is a rare sight here.

It's a paradox of the Central African Republic which the UN ranks as the second least developed in the world.

Nearly half of the population is in a state of (¹   ) emergency despite millions of hectares of arable land.   5

But things could be changing thanks to some private investors like Jan-Luc Tete who was born in Central African Republic.

For the (²   ) years, in the fertile region of Lobaye, this business man has been betting on what he calls 'regenerative' agriculture.

Based on traditional techniques, it uses practically no fertiliser.   10

He sees great agribusiness potential in a country that has (³   ) decades of armed conflict and poor governance.

"We have available land, we have an exceptional climate, we have quite exceptional market conditions, and in fact we decided to create a champion of sustainable agriculture because it allows us to have an agriculture that conserves the soil and it allows us to 15 have extremely low production costs, which are the necessary conditions to be able to start an agriculture here."

Land use is negotiated with the village chiefs. And (⁴   ) percent of profits are fed back into the community, some of which went into building a school.

But few investors have taken the plunge in this initiative.   20

The Palme d'Or company, which is a producer of palm oil, is still the only major investor.

"We have been witnessing this for years, through food aid, which never develops the sector, on the contrary it makes us lazier, it inculcates in our heads a mentality of the assisted, the people who always needs to reach out for help. But when it's the private sector that takes charge, it's something else. It's a question of partnership between 25 those who are going to invest and the producers, and everyone wins."

This investment drive is also (⁵   ) the manufacturing of processed products, such as palm oil soaps, to better protect the industry, and its workers, from fluctuations in the price of raw materials.

But the cultivation of palm oil in the region has faced criticism from environmentalists, 30 who have warned that it is a threat to biodiversity and driver of deforestation.

In a country where two thirds of the food staple cassava is imported, developing this sector could help to stop people having to choose between eating and thriving.

≫ Exchanging Ideas and Thoughts ----------------------

Practice the conversation with your partner. Think about how you can develop the conversation further.

A: I think 中央アフリカ共和国の問題について学んだのははじめてです。

_____

B: 普段アフリカの国のことはあまり気にしないもんね。

_____

A: Honestly, I don't even know much about issues in Asian countries.

B: Well, that's an interesting point. Many of SDGs are too common in Japan, I think.

A: That's right. We take things like social infrastructure, educational opportunities, and medical care for granted.

B: We should appreciate the safe and sound society in Japan. And of course, we have to think about what we can do to assist for foreign countries.

 Further Activity

(1) Visit the following websites to learn about **Goal 2** and **food industry**. Take notes and share some of the most interesting information you find with your classmates. **(2)** Using your own key words and/or phrases, try Cinii Research or a similar information retrieval system to find some books and articles that are of interest to you. Compare your list of books and articles with your classmates' lists.

Goal 2

SDGs and Food industry

12 Dam and Plastic Waste
― ダムとプラゴミ ―

このユニットでは、目標 12「つくる責任使う責任」の内容を踏まえて、ゴミ問題と再生可能エネルギーについて考えます。世界で生産されまたゴミとして廃棄されるプラスチックの総量や、アフリカ大陸で 8 番目に大きな湖であるキボ湖での水力発電とプラゴミ問題の実例について学び、持続可能な社会の実現に向けた課題について知識を深めます。

▶▶ Warm Up Quizzes

Learn about SDGs' Goal 12 by completing the following statements.

1.【figures】 Our _____ on natural resources is increasing, rising over 65% globally from 2000 to 2019.

   (A) **reliance**　　　(B) **rely**　　　(C) **relied**　　　(D) **relying**

2.【fact】 Vast majority of the world's electronic waste is not being _____ managed.

   (A) **safe**　　　(B) **safety**　　　(C) **safest**　　　(D) **safely**

3.【fact】 The COVID-19 pandemic _____ the global pollution crisis, in particular plastics pollution.

   (A) **aggravate**　　　(B) **aggravated**　　　(C) **aggravation**　　　(D) **aggravating**

4.【fact】 In 2021, a new global regime for _____ trade of plastic wastes for better transparency and tracing was established.

   (A) **control**　　　(B) **controlling**　　　(C) **controls**　　　(D) **to be controlled**

>> Reading Activities ···················· 🔊 Audio 2-09

Read the following passage about community acceptance.

❶ One of the biggest problems facing the world in the coming decades is how to reduce the huge amount of plastic waste that is produced every year. [1] Scarily, between 2010 and 2020 the global production of plastics increased from 270 million tonnes to 376 million tonnes. Whilst every year more than 12 million ⁵ tonnes of plastic waste end up floating in rivers, lakes, and oceans in every corner of the Earth. The consequence for marine life is clear, yet when macro-plastics degrade into micro-plastics, they can easily contaminate the food chain which can result in severe threats to human health via inhalation and ingestion. ₁₀

face　直面する
decade　10年
scarily　恐ろしいことに

end up ~ing　～することになる
float　浮かぶ
consequence　結果
degrade　劣化する
inhalation　吸入
ingestion　摂取

❷ In Africa, the number of plastic waste is expected to reach 165 million tonnes by 2030. [2] The number of plastic waste in African waters is expected to reach 17 million tonnes by the end of 2022, triple the size since 2010.

triple　3倍にする

❸ Lake Kivu, which straddles the border of Rwanda, and the ₁₅ Democratic Republic of the Congo is one of the many African waterways where the increase in plastic has become a dangerous hazard for marine and human life. The freshwater lake with a maximum length of 89 km and a maximum depth of 480 metres is the 8th largest lake on the continent and the 18th deepest in ₂₀ the world.

Lake Kivu　キブ湖
straddle　またがる
border　国境
Rwanda　ルワンダ
the Democratic Republic of the Congo　コンゴ民主共和国
freshwater　淡水
continent　大陸

❹ As well as home to necessary marine life that supports communities around its shores, Lake Kivu is also an important source of hydroelectric power for the region. [3] The Ruzizi Dam, first opened in 1958, and the attached power stations are ₂₅ expected to provide 287 megawatts of generating power by the middle of the 2020s. Yet the issue of plastic waste in Lake Kivu has become a huge concern that has already caused disruption to the power plants.

hydroelectric power　水力発電
region　地域
the Ruzizi Dam　ルジジダム
concern　懸念
disruption　妨害, 混乱
sheer number of　非常に多くの
discard　廃棄する

❺ In January 2020 the sheer number of plastic waste discarded ₃₀ in Lake Kivu caused major problems for the hydroelectric power stations. [4] The result is that the power stations have seen a 20-megawatt energy deficit, which has led to power outages in nearby cities. A massive rubbish patch measuring 14 metres in depth caused one of the power stations' four turbines to break 35 down. The problem remains however, that every time one plastic bottle is removed from Lake Kivu, three more bottles are thrown in. Until that trend is reversed, the lake and other African waterways are fighting a losing battle against an endemic of plastic waste. 40

deficit 損失
outage 供給停止
rubbish patch ゴ
ミの塊

reverse 逆転する
a losing battle 無
駄な抵抗、負け戦
endemic 地域特有
の問題

Reading Comprehension 1

Read through the text and choose the correct answer.

1. What is NOT mentioned in the first paragraph?

　a) The amount of plastic waste worldwide has increased rapidly.

　b) Reducing the amount of plastic waste is one of the most important challenges for sustainable development.

　c) A significant proportion of plastic waste is discarded in rivers and oceans.

　d) Plastic waste has more impact on marine life than on human health.

2. What does the third paragraph mainly describe?

　a) The geographic feature of Lake Kivu

　b) Hydropower generation capacity of the Ruzizi Dam

　c) Contamination level of Lake Kivu

　d) Biodiversity of Lake Kivu

3. What can you infer from the fourth and fifth paragraphs?

　a) There are some non-profit organizations working on plastic waste issues at Lake Kivu.

　b) The Ruzizi Dam is no longer in operation due to damages caused by plastic wastes.

　c) Fishery at Lake Kivu is important for local people's life.

　d) The amount of plastic bottles thrown in Lake Kivu has been decreasing.

4. In which positions from [1] to [4], does the following sentence best belong?
　"Yet, a significant proportion of plastic that ends up in African waterways are produced outside of the continent."

　a) [1]　　　　　　　**b)** [2]　　　　　　　**c)** [3]　　　　　　　**d)** [4]

Reading Comprehension 2

Answer the following questions in a complete sentence.

1. Why is Lake Kivu mentioned in the passage?

It is mentioned to (give / the issue of / an example / plastic waste / of).

_____

2. What was the damage caused by plastic waste to the hydroelectric power station?

_____

⊙ Video Activities

Watch the video and answer the following questions.

Check the facts in the video: True or False Questions

Circle **T** if the statement is true or **F** if it is false.

1. Lake Kivu is surrounded by mountains. [**T** / **F**]

2. It rarely rains around Lake Kivu through the year. [**T** / **F**]

3. A problem of plastic waste at Lake Kivu has not been addressed until recently. [**T** / **F**]

4. Divers' effort to remove plastic waste has not been so effective. [**T** / **F**]

Watch the video and choose the correct answer. Read the script if necessary.

1. What is true about the video?

  a) The dam construction project destroyed forests around the lake.

  b) Local people around the lake need schools and hospitals the most.

  c) The government announced support for cleaning the lake.

  d) There is a local company working on waste issues.

2. What is Byumanine Mubalama's problem?

  a) He does not get paid for his service.

  b) He does not have proper tools for cleaning plastic waste.

  c) His family members are suffering from poverty.

  d) His company does not have financial source to employ new staff members.

3. What does Nicola's company do?

   a) Selling cleaning tools

   b) Repairing boats

   c) Producing utensils from rubbish

   d) Delivering foods and medicines

Watch the video and complete the script.   📶 **Audio 2-10**

   It's a pile up. In the Ruzizi Dam in the very south of Lake Kivu thousands of bottles, jerry cans and plastic packaging block the power station's turbines. The mountainous terrain and heavy rains here on the border between the Democratic Republic of the Congo and Rwanda carry in waste from (¹   ) kilometres away.

   "All the waste we throw into the lake or the river comes to wash up here. (²   ) 5 where we throw it."

   This is not a new problem. Byumanine Mubalama has been cleaning up on his boat for 13 years, but with the sheer amount of waste it is an uphill battle.

   "Everyday there is rubbish that I have to clean. I don't even have the tools to do it. It's a real problem."   10

   And there is even more than meets the eye. (³   ) the waste reaches down to a depth of 14 metres. At the Ruzizi Hydroelectric Plant the largest in the eastern DRC, a turbine broke down in January. Divers tried to tackle the blockage to no avail.

   "This is a 6.3-megawatt unit out of the total of 30 megawatts that we can produce you understand, and that 6.3 is not available."   15

Due to other (⁴   ) because of the waste, a total of 20 megawatts is missing from the grid. This means that the electricity supplied to the towns of Bukavu and Uvira is restricted. Some are calling for penalties for 20 those who throw their rubbish in the lake. There are also efforts to set up collections of household waste. Nicole Menemene runs a small private waste recovery business in the area.

   "There are some households that call us to go and collect their plastic waste from their 25 homes. We also do (⁵   ) sometimes in the rivers or on the road. So, we make sure that the waste does not reach the lake."

Menemene's company transforms collected rubbish into objects both useful and beautiful. Baskets, flowerpots, bins and stools. But with only 10 employees it's a drop in an ocean of waste. This small company has big dreams though. One day it hopes projects like this will cut pollution in Lake Kivu by 90 percent. 30

» Exchanging Ideas and Thoughts · · · · · · · · · · · · · ·

Practice the conversation with your partner. Think about how you can develop the conversation further.

A: 何トンものプラゴミの所為でクリーンエネルギーの発電所がうまく機能していないのが分かったよ。

_____

B: ゴミがもたらすダメージを見過ごすわけにはいかないね。

_____

A: You're right. I am wondering who actually constructed a dam in the heart of African continent.

B: That's an interesting point. Maybe, an international construction company did.

A: Often times such construction project is financially supported by developed countries.

B: Yes. Maybe Japan did. I've heard that the Japanese government and some Japanese companies have helped construct infrastructure, like railways, in a developing country.

 Further Activity

(1) Visit the following websites to learn more about **Goal 7** and **12**. Take notes and share some of the most interesting information you find with your classmates. (2) Using your own key words and/or phrases, try Cinii Research or a similar information retrieval system to find some books and articles that are of interest to you. Compare your list of books and articles with your classmates' lists.

Goal 7   Goal 12

13 Child Labor Issues
— 児童労働問題 —

© Dietmar Temps / Shutterstock.com

世界では多くの子供たちが日々の生活をしていくために仕事をすることを余儀なくされています。児童労働は、貧困、健康、衛生、生活環境、教育などが関係する深刻な問題です。このユニットでは、目標4「質の高い教育をみんなに」と目標8「働きがいも経済成長も」を踏まえて、児童労働についての知識を深め国際社会がどのように問題について取り組むべきか考えます。

≫ Warm Up Quizzes -

Learn about SDGs' Goal 4 and 8 by completing the following statements.

1.【Goal】 Goal 4 aims to ensure quality education and promote lifelong _____ opportunities for all.

(A) **learns**   (B) **learning**   (C) **learned**   (D) **to learn**

2.【Target (Goal 4)】 By 2030, ensure that all girls and boys have _____ to quality early childhood development, care and pre-primary education.

(A) **accessing**   (B) **access**   (C) **accesses**   (D) **accessed**

3.【Goal】 Goal 8 aims to promote _____ employment and decent work for all.

(A) **productive**   (B) **produce**   (C) **producing**   (D) **production**

4.【Target (Goal 8)】 By 2020, substantially reduce the proportion of youth not in employment, education or _____.

(A) **trained**   (B) **a trainer**   (C) **a trainee**   (D) **training**

United Nations Department of Economic and Social Affairs Sustainable Development   https://sdgs.un.org/goals

❯❯ Reading Activities ···················· 🔊 Audio 2-11

Read the following passage.

❶ According to the UN Convention on the Rights of the Child, everyone under 18 years of age is generally considered a "child" and therefore has the rights of a child. Some articles in the convention are about education. Every child has the right to access education. Primary education should be complimentary, and ₅ children's human dignity should be respected in schools. Education at schools should foster each child's personality and talent (Article 28). Children should be encouraged to respect their parents, their culture, and other cultures through education (Article 29). Children's engagement in work that could harm their health or ₁₀ education should not be allowed by the government (Article 32).

❷ One thing that can deprive children of their right to an education is child labor. Child labor is different from doing household chores to help family members or getting pocket money for taking part in an easy task appropriate for a child. ₁₅ Rather, child labor usually refers to full-time work with significant responsibility that is not particularly designed for children. Often, child labor involves a horrible, unhygienic working environment, insufficient wages, and high social and psychological pressure. It not only deprives children from ₂₀ opportunities for education, but it also has a negative impact on children's physical, social, and psychological development. Since a child laborer usually has little opportunity to gain new skills or knowledge from their work, they cannot escape the low-income cycle. As a result, their poor quality of life does not ₂₅ measurably improve throughout their adult life.

❸ Sadly, even in today's world, child labor is all too common. The International Labor Organization (ILO) reported that there were about 152 million working children in 2017, equating to one in ten of the total children population at that time. The ratio is ₃₀ the highest in sub-Saharan Africa where one in four children,

the UN Convention on the Rights of the Child 児童の権利に関する国連条約
article 条項
primary education 初等教育
complimentary 無料
human dignity 人間の尊厳
harm 害する
deprive 奪う
household chore 家事
appropriate ふさわしい
unhygienic 不衛生な
insufficient 不十分な
wage 賃金
deprive 奪う
impact 影響
low-income 低収入
as a result 結果として
measurably 分かるほど、明らかに
sadly 悲しいことに、残念ながら
ILO 国際労働機関
equate to ～に等しい
ratio 割合、比率

aging from 5 to 17, is a victim to child labor.

❹ [1] Some of the UN Sustainable Development Goals (SDGs) target a child's well-being and child labor. Goal 8, for instance, is about "Decent work and Economic Growth," with one of its targets being to prohibit harmful child labor, such as child soldiers or the enslavement of children. [2] It also aims to bring all forms of child labor to an end by 2025. Another SDG target related to child labor is Goal 16, titled "Peace, Justice, and Strong Institutions." [3] Not all child labor always involves physical violence or torture, but there is no doubt that child labor is a form of exploitation because it robs children of the time needed to receive education, which is a basic right for all children. [4]

❺ Among the issues facing contemporary international society is the lack of international consensus or legal regulation of the minimum age limit for children to work full time. It is reported that the total number of child laborers has decreased by about 134 million from 2000 to 2016; however, it is apparent that much remains to be done to fulfill the SDG targets mentioned above.

victim 犠牲者

target 目標 [対象] にする
decent work 働きがいのある人間らしい仕事
enslavement 奴隷化

torture 拷問、痛めつけること
exploitation 搾取
rob A of B AからBを奪う
contemporary 現代の
consensus 一致した意見、総意
legal regulation 法的規制

Reading Comprehension 1

Read through the text and choose the correct answer.

1. What is true about child labor?

    a) Children can gain job experience and learn new skills through child labor.

    b) Doing household chores for family members is a form of child labor.

    c) Usually jobs or tasks for child laborers are designed for young children, not for adults.

    d) Children's physical and psychological development is hampered due to child labor.

2. What is NOT mentioned as a problem of child labor?

    a) Low income

    b) Poor hygiene

    c) Night shift

    d) High pressure

3. In which positions from [1] to [4], does the following sentence best belong?

"One of its targets is to put an end to any form of abuse, exploitation, and violence against children."

a) [1]　　　　　**b)** [2]　　　　　**c)** [3]　　　　　**d)** [4]

Reading Comprehension 2

Answer the following questions in a complete sentence.

1. Why it is difficult for international society to tackle child labor issues?

Because (age limit / about / no / there is / international regulation).

_____

2. According to an article in the UN convention, what two things are negatively affected by child labor?

_____

⊙ Video Activities ---

Watch the video and answer the following questions.

Check the facts in the video: True or False Questions

 Circle **T** if the statement is true or **F** if it is false.

1. The video is mostly about how parents protect their children from child labor.　　[**T** / **F**]

2. This is the first case that the child labor issue is reported through the media.　　[**T** / **F**]

3. Sixty eight adults who employed children were arrested.　　[**T** / **F**]

4. Non-Governmental Organizations (NGOs) have helped to address the child labor issue. [**T** / **F**]

Watch the video and choose the correct answer. Read the script if necessary.

1. What is one of the major industries in Ivory Coast?

　a) Child trafficking

　b) Cocoa plantation

　c) Car manufacturing

　d) E-waste recycling

2. What is indicated in the video?

   a) Pressure from overseas made the government tackle the child labor issue.

   b) Financial assistance from foreign countries helped to solve the problem.

   c) An international conference was set to be held to investigate the child labor issue.

   d) Many local families wanted their children to work as child laborers.

3. What is the key to let child laborers talk about their problems?

   a) Nutritious meals

   b) Clean clothes and bed

   c) Friendly communication

   d) Spacious room and toys

Watch the video and complete the script.   Audio 2-12

Instead of attending school, these children in the Ivory Coast sort through cocoa beans on a plantation. Child labour in the industry is a scourge the country is trying to stamp out.

In early May, a high-profile police operation received wide media coverage.

For two days, (¹   ) of officers were mobilised in the western Soubre region to ₅ root out children working. Around 68 were found.

"We've been trying to (²   ) for a long time. But as long as you don't send strong signals, as well as punish people who employ children in dangerous work one by one, it will always continue. So we have to send signals."

   (³   ) people were sentenced to prison for child trafficking as a result of the ₁₀ operation.

The Ivory Coast is the world's largest cocoa producer. NGOs have been highlighting the plight of child labourers for decades.

But only recently has the country experienced pressure from Western consumers demanding ethical practices.   ₁₅

In just two years, some (⁴   ) children have been removed from plantations.

Many of them have found refuge in this centre in Soubre.

"I stopped going to school when I was 10 years old. When my parents didn't have enough money, I went out and helped them by working in the field."

Poverty is the main cause behind child exploitation.   ₂₀

According to the World Bank, over 2.5 million people working in the cocoa industry live below the poverty line.

"When we welcome the children, we smile a lot to gain their trust... and during the exchanges as well. And we initially listen. This allows us to detect whether the child is being trafficked or not, or if they are working or not."

Parents are then invited to the centre to discuss the situation further. This mediation work helps improve the schooling rate of children in families working in the industry.

In serious cases involving (^{5}) or forced labour, the children remain at the centre where they attend school.

≫ Exchanging Ideas and Thoughts ---------------

Practice the conversation with your partner. Think about how you can develop the conversation further.

A: 日本に児童労働者がいると思いますか？

_____

B: いいえ、今まで一度も聞いたことがないです。

_____

A: I cannot imagine young children working full-time for a living.

B: They cannot get out of it because they do not have enough chances to learn new skills or knowledge.

A: That is a serious problem. I am wondering what we can do to help.

B: Let's look to NPOs or NGOs tackling the issue.

 Further Activity

(1) Visit the following website to learn about **Goal 4**, **8**, and **16**. Take notes and share some of the most interesting information you find with your classmates. (2) Using your own key words and/or phrases, try Cinii Research or a similar information retrieval system to find some books and articles that are of interest to you. Compare your list of books and articles with your classmates' lists.

Goal 4   Goal 8   Goal 16

14 Used Phones Recycled into Works of Art

— リサイクルアート —

© PhotoChur / Shutterstock.com

芸術と持続可能な開発目標（SDGs）は一見関連が薄いように思えます。しかし実際には環境問題を反映した芸術作品や、廃棄物を用いたリサイクルアート、芸術活動の場として使われなくなった施設を再生するなど、様々な芸術に関する活動が行われています。このユニットでは、目標 15「陸の豊かさも守ろう」を踏まえて、環境芸術やリサイクルアートについて学び、芸術を通した問題喚起の重要性について考えます。

≫ Warm Up Quizzes

Learn about SDGs' Goal 14 by completing the following statements.

1. 【Goal】 Protect, restore and promote sustainable use of terrestrial _____.

   (A) **ecosystems**　　(B) **subsystems**　　(C) **operating systems** (D) **cybersystems**

2. 【Target】 By 2020, promote the implementation of sustainable management of all types of _____.

   (A) **quests**　　(B) **harvests**　　(C) **tempests**　　(D) **forests**

3. 【Target】 By 2030, ensure the conservation of mountain ecosystems, including their _____.

   (A) **biodiversity**　　(B) **obesity**　　(C) **propensity**　　(D) **intensity**

4. 【Figure】 Ten million hectares of forests are _____ every year.

   (A) **destroying**　　(B) **destroy**　　(C) **destroyed**　　(D) **destruction**

United Nations Department of Economic and Social Affairs Sustainable Development　https://sdgs.un.org/goals

⏩ Reading Activities ⸺⸺⸺⸺⸺ 🔊 Audio 2-13

Read the following passage about art and SDGs.

❶ Fields of art or artistic activities seem to have the weakest link with Sustainable Development Goals (SDGs). However, some artists reflect social or global issues in their artworks. One such art form is known as "environmental art." Generally, environmental art does not refer to paintings of beautiful scenery 5 or sculptures displayed outside such as in parks or on sidewalks for public viewing. One of the common features of environmental art is that it takes the natural environment as the medium. More importantly, it is usually inspired by the natural environment and delivers some message to viewers so that they can think 10 about the importance of nature or the harmonious coexistence of nature and humans. In this sense, the famous carving of four presidents of the United States on Mt. Rushmore in South Dakota is not categorized as environmental art because, although it takes the mountain surface as its medium and is presented in 15 the natural environment, it has little to do with the way we view the environment or environmental issues.

❷ Holding art festivals based on SDGs is one direct way to connect art and SDGs. There have been a number of such festivals in Japan. Pictures painted by local residents, especially 20 school kids, are often displayed and they are supposed to evoke an environment-friendly spirit among local community.

❸ Turning remnants of old facilities once used for resource exploitation or some other purposes into an art center is another example of direct connection between art and SDGs. [1] One 25 typical example is the Zollverein coal mine in Essen, Germany. [2] The coal mine has more than 200 Bauhaus style facilities across an area of one million square meters. Bauhaus means "building house" in German, and the Bauhaus was a German art school established in 1919 and disbanded in 1933. [3] Due to its functional 30 beauty, a group of Zollverein coal mine facilities was designated

link 関連

reflect 反映する
artwork 芸術作品
environmental art
環境芸術
refer to ～のことを
言う
painting 絵画
sculpture 彫刻 (作
品)、彫像
sidewalk 歩道
medium 媒体、素材
deliver 伝える

coexistence 共存
carving 彫刻

South Dakota サウ
スダコタ州
mountain surface
山肌

have little to do with~
～とほとんど関係ない

hold 開催する
resident 住人

evoke 喚起する

remnant 残された物
exploitation 開発

typical 典型的な
coal mine 炭鉱
the Zollverein coal
mine ツォルフェ
ライン炭鉱
Bauhaus style バ
ウハウス様式の

disband 解散する
designate 指定する

a World Heritage Site in 2001. With a number of modern artworks sporadically displayed in the area, it has been redeveloped as an art center. [4] There are also similar examples in Japan. Kanazawa Citizen's Art Center in Ishikawa, a spinning mill turned into a 35 gallery and theater, and Maizuru Red Brick Park in Kyoto, a pre-war Japanese navy warehouse area developed into a park and art space, are among them.

❹ Recycled art is yet another example. This type of art uses any discarded materials such as plastic bottles, empty cans, metals, 40 tires, electronic devices, clothes, and so on. Recycled art not only makes people pay attention to waste problems but also directly contributes to reducing trash to be landfilled or incinerated. It is true that the total amount of waste used for artistic purposes accounts for a very tiny proportion, but we cannot 45 ignore the power it has to raise our awareness of environmental issues, the importance of recycling, and a sustainable society.

World Heritage
 Site 世界遺産
sporadically いた
 るところに
spinning mill 紡績
 工場
navy 海軍
warehouse 倉庫

discarded 廃棄された
empty 空の
device 装置、機器

landfill 埋め立てる
incinerate 焼却する

account for 占める
tiny とても小さい

Reading Comprehension 1

Read through the text and choose the correct answer.

1. What is true about art and artistic activities?

　a) SDGs-related themes are now popular among young artists.

　b) It is one of areas that has practically no connection with SDGs.

　c) SDGs related issues can be reflected to artworks.

　d) Many artists devote themselves to social activities related to environmental issues.

2. What is NOT mentioned about environmental art?

　a) A picture of beautiful mountains or forests is the typical example of environmental art.

　b) It uses the natural environment as the medium.

　c) It is usually presented in a natural environment.

　d) It is created to send important messages to viewers.

3. What is the passage about?

　a) Artistic activities by young artists and their artworks

　b) Examples of SDGs-related artworks or activities

　c) Description of one of the world famous sculptures

　d) How to set the price on a particular painting

4. In which positions from [1] to [4], does the following sentence best belong?

"The term is now often used to refer to designs that combine aesthetics with functionalism."

a) [1]   **b)** [2]   **c)** [3]   **d)** [4]

Reading Comprehension 2

Answer the following questions in a complete sentence.

1. What is one of the common features of environmental art?

(the medium / usually takes / as / the natural environment / environmental art).

_____

2. How can out-of-use buildings be used for art?

_____

▶ Video Activities

Watch the video and answer the following questions.

Check the facts in the video: True or False Questions

 Circle **T** if the statement is true or **F** if it is false.

1. The video is about a self-reliant artist who works all by himself.   [**T** / **F**]

2. The artist, Mounou Koffi, has an educational background in art.   [**T** / **F**]

3. Mounou Koffi has had art exhibitions in foreign countries.   [**T** / **F**]

4. Artworks in the video are basically free and people can take them if they are interested in recycled art.   [**T** / **F**]

Watch the video and choose the correct answer. Read the script if necessary.

1. What is the medium used for artworks in the video?

    a) Mobile phone keyboards

    b) Computer monitors

    c) Discarded canvases

    d) Human cut hair

2. What is indicated in the video?

  a) Recycled art contributes to the development of local agriculture.

  b) The artist does not create artworks for profits.

  c) Local community helps the artist by providing grants.

  d) Creating recycled artworks provide jobs for local people.

3. What is an important aspect of creating artworks from discarded materials?

  a) Making friends all over the world

  b) Saving endangered animals in Africa

  c) Reporting facts and figures about climate crisis

  d) Raising awareness toward recycling, environment, and sustainable society

Watch the video and complete the script.   Audio 2-14

At first glance, a patchwork. But on closer inspection it's not made of fabric, but of mobile phones. Dozens of keyboards from (¹   ), sewn together and used as a canvas, from which Mounou Désiré Koffi makes his works. His unusual medium makes this young Ivorian artist stand out.

  "Why recycling? Because I didn't want to limit my work only to painting, to the medium ₅ of painting, to express myself just in that way. I wanted to bring something new. And I think the mobile phone is the tool that we're most attached to. Most of my work is about life, about people, so basically how people are in society."

Koffi started scouring the streets and rubbish dumps to (²   ) old phones after graduating from the Abidjan Art School. These days, he has a whole team on the lookout ₁₀ for him. The more they bring in, the more they'll get paid. And in a country that hardly sorts its waste Koffi, hopes to change attitudes, by (³   ) about recycling.

  "I think that just the act of collecting old phones, of breathing new life into so-called waste, people say to themselves 'uh-huh!' In fact, these things that have been thrown away, that don't work anymore, can be made into something new, it can contribute ₁₅ something."

The collected keyboards are passed onto these seamstresses to be assembled. Koffi is the artistic brains behind the operation, thinking up new (⁴   ). One of his latest series, "Life here " acts as a portrait of the daily lives of the people of Abidjan. Some of his pieces sell for up to $1,500. After exhibitions in Morocco, Belgium and France, his latest ₂₀ show is right here at home. The 28-year-old has caught the attention of the art world.

"Doing something useful for humanity is always encouraging and making it pretty... and raising awareness is even better."

"The canvas is an innovative one since he works on canvases that are rubbish, in fact, he breathes new life into these canvases and that brings even more to African contemporary art." 25

Koffi's works will (5   ) until July, you could say he's got recycling down to a fine art.

▶▶ Exchanging Ideas and Thoughts ·················

Practice the conversation with your partner. Think about how you can develop the conversation further.

A: 芸術祭や展示会に行ったことはありますか?

_____

B: Yes, I have. 地元の町で去年の夏にその地域の芸術祭が開催されました。

_____

A: What was it like?

B: They displayed many paintings and some sculptures made by local people.

A: I see. Did it have any theme or something?

B: I think it was about environmental issues or community development, but as far as I have seen, visitors didn't take it too seriously.

 Further Activity

(1) Visit the following website to learn about **Goal 15** and **recycled art**. Take notes and share some of the most interesting information you find with your classmates. (2) Using your own key words and/or phrases, try Cinii Research or a similar information retrieval system to find some books and articles that are of interest to you. Compare your list of books and articles with your classmates' lists.

Goal 15   Recycled Art

15 Review Quiz

❯❯ Vocabulary Check -

Match each word with its meaning.

Nouns 1

1	objectives	( )	5	drought	( )	9	option	( )
2	prosperity	( )	6	wheat	( )	10	device	( )
3	decade	( )	7	investment	( )			
4	consumption	( )	8	measure	( )			

a 倉庫	b 干ばつ	c 繁栄	d 装置、機器	e 対策	f 海岸
g 選択肢	h 目標	i 小麦	j 10年	k 投資	l 消費

Nouns 2

11	habitat	( )	15	profit	( )	19	durability	( )
12	fabric	( )	16	driver	( )	20	waste	( )
13	border	( )	17	continent	( )			
14	precipitation	( )	18	sculpture	( )			

a 国境	b 彫刻、彫像	c 大陸	d 要因、動機	e 収入	f 降雨
g ゴミ	h 織物	i 利益	j 状態	k 生息地	l 耐久性

Verbs 1

21	rely	( )	25	decompose	( )	29	minimize	( )
22	earn	( )	26	absorb	( )	30	tackle	( )
23	melt	( )	27	monitor	( )			
24	apply	( )	28	exceed	( )			

a 取り組む	b 最小にする	c 適用する、利用する	d 経験する	e 超える	f 漂う、漂流する
g 吸収する	h 稼ぐ、得る	i 頼る、〜による	j 観察する、監視する	k 分解する	l 溶かす

Verbs 2

31 incinerate	( )	35 face	( )	39 designate	( )
32 account for	( )	36 affect	( )	40 reverse	( )
33 evoke	( )	37 discard	( )		
34 disband	( )	38 reflect	( )		

a 解散する	b 焼却する	c 逆転する	d 示す	e 相続する	f 指定する
g 反映する	h 直面する	i 占める	j 廃棄する	k 影響する	l 喚起する

≫ SDGs' Goals and Targets --------------------------------

(41)【Goal】 Goal 2 aims to end hunger, achieve food security, improve nutrition and ___ sustainable agriculture.

A. promotes   B. promoting   C. promoted   D. promote

(42)【Target】 By 2030, double the agricultural ___ and incomes of small-scale food producers.

A. productivity   B. produce   C. producing   D. productive

(43)【Goal】 Goal 4 aims to ensure quality education and promote lifelong ___ opportunities for all.

A. learns   B. to learn   C. learned   D. learning

(44)【Target】 By 2030, ensure that all girls and boys have ___ to quality early childhood development, care and pre-primary education.

A. access   B. accessing   C. accesses   D. accessed

(45)【Goal】 Goal 7 aims to ensure access to affordable, ___, sustainable and modern energy for all.

A. reasonable   B. redundant   C. responsive   D. reliable

(46)【Target】 By 2030, increase substantially the share of ___ energy in the global energy mix.

A. renewing   B. renew   C. renewable   D. renewed

(47) 【Target】 By 2020, substantially reduce the proportion of youth not in employment, education or ___.

   A. trained   B. training   C. a trainee   D. a trainer

(48) 【Goal】 Goal 8 aims to promote ___ employment and decent work for all.

   A. produce   B. productive   C. producing   D. production

(49) 【Goal】 Goal 9 aims to build strong infrastructure and support ___.

   A. innovated   B. innovation   C. innovative   D. innovates

(50) 【Target】 Support domestic technology development, research and innovation ___ developing countries.

   A. in   B. at   C. on   D. between

(51) 【Goal】 Goal 10 aims to ___ inequality within and among countries.

   A. change   B. bring reduce   C. reduce   D. increase

(52) 【Target】 "Progressively ___ and sustain income growth of the bottom 40 percent of the population at a rate higher than the national average."

   A. achieve   B. form   C. make   D. organize

(53) 【Goal】 Goal 11 aims to ___ human cities and settlements safe and sustainable.

   A. adjust   B. develop   C. leave   D. make

(54) 【Target】 Strengthen efforts to ___ the world's cultural and natural heritage.

   A. protecting   B. protection   C. protector   D. protect

(55) 【Goal】 Goal 12 aims to ___ sustainable consumption and production patterns.

   A. ensure   B. insure   C. decide   D. discuss

(56) 【Target】 By 2030, Achieve the sustainable management and ___ use of natural resources."

   A. perfect   B. finalized   C. organized   D. efficient

(57) 【Goal】 Goal 13 aims to take urgent action to combat climate change and its ___.

A. insufficiency   B. importance   C. inequalities   D. impacts

Unit
15

(58) 【Target】 ___ resilience to climate-related hazards and natural disasters in all countries.

A. Strengthen   B. Weaken   C. Shorten   D. Lengthen

(59) 【Goal 14】 Goal 14 "Life Below Water" aims to conserve marine resources and use them ___.

A. sustaining   B. sustains   C. sustainably   D. sustainment

(60) 【Goal 15】 Goal 5 aims to protect, restore and promote sustainable use of terrestrial ___.

A. ecosystems   B. subsystems   C. operating systems   D. cybersystems

JPCA

日本出版著作権協会
http://www.jpca.jp.net/

本書は日本出版著作権協会（JPCA）が委託管理する著作物です。
複写（コピー）・複製、その他著作物の利用については、事前に JPCA（電話 03-3812-9424、e-mail:info@e-jpca.com）の許諾を得て下さい。なお、無断でコピー・スキャン・デジタル化等の複製をすることは著作権法上の例外を除き、著作権法違反となります。

SDGs and Challenges We Face
映像メディアで考える SDGs

2023 年 4 月 10 日　初版第 1 刷発行
2024 年 4 月 10 日　初版第 2 刷発行

編 著 者　山本五郎／Jonathan D. Brown／Jaime Selwood

発 行 者　森　信久
発 行 所　株式会社　松 柏 社
　　　　　〒102-0072　東京都千代田区飯田橋 1−6−1
　　　　　TEL　03 (3230) 4813（代表）
　　　　　FAX　03 (3230) 4857
　　　　　http://www.shohakusha.com
　　　　　e-mail: info@shohakusha.com

装　　幀　小島トシノブ（NONdesign）
本文レイアウト・組版・印刷・製本　株式会社木元省美堂
ISBN978-4-88198-781-0
略　　号 = 781

Copyright © 2023 by Goro Yamamoto, Jonathan D. Brown, and Jaime Selwood

本書を無断で複写・複製することを禁じます。
落丁・乱丁は送料小社負担にてお取り替え致します。